Parasites

An Epidemic
in Disguise

Written and Compiled by
Stanley Weinberger, C.M.T.

© 1993 by Stanley Weinberger
Healing Within Products
P.O. Box 1013
Larkspur, CA 94977-1013

Telephone: (415) 454-6677
FAX: (415) 454-6659

1st Printing 1993
2nd Printing 1994
3rd Printing 1997

Parasites: An Epidemic in Disguise can be purchased
at most health food stores and bookstores.
For mail orders, see order form on pages 71-72.

Front cover photographs by Institute of Parasitic Diseases, Phoenix, AZ
Back cover photograph by American Biologics, Chula Vista, CA.
Cover Design by Allen Crider, Fairfax, CA

ISBN 0-9616184-8-5

Printed in the U.S.A.

Note to the Reader

Parasites: An Epidemic in Disguise does not claim to substitute for a physician's care, nor does it advocate specific solutions to individual problems. The physicians and experts providing the enclosed information have substantiated their claims as well as possible, considering that data on health and nutrition are subject to change as we learn more.

Before following the self-help advice given in this book, readers are earnestly urged to give careful consideration to the nature of their particular health problem and to consult a competent physician if they are in any doubt.

This book should not be regarded as a substitute for professional medical treatment. Every care has been taken to ensure accuracy of the content. Still, the author and publisher cannot accept legal responsibility for any problem arising out of the methods described in this book.

Acknowledgments

We thank the Bradford Research Institute (BRI®), Chula Vista, California, manufacturers of projection microscopy equipment, for providing the images used on the back cover and the color insert.

Nearly two decades of research and development at BRI have culminated in the most advanced variable projection multi-phase optical microscopy system available. The Bradford Variable Projection Microscopy (BVPM™) video enhanced system achieves the highest variable magnification with outstanding resolution, contrast, and clarity — capable of resolving detail of less than 0.15 microns with magnification from 40X to over 15,000X.

Since 1978, BRI has pioneered the concept of Oxidology, the study of reactive oxygen toxic species in health and disease as a precise medical subspecialty. BRI research members worldwide have confirmed what Dr. Bradford first asserted — the importance of oxidative mechanisms in the full spectrum of pathology.

The development of the BVPM has made possible the correlaton of pathology with the dynamics of peripheral blood morphology, yielding unique insights into clinical and subclinical mechanisms. With digital imaging, the BVPM can process, enhance, store and retrieve digital images, providing photographic quality hard images (as used in this book). The BVPM microscopy system is helping define the future of science in health care.

We also thank the Institute of Parasitic Diseases in Phoenix, Arizona for the use of their images on the front cover and in the insert in this book.

Table of Contents

The first major nationwide survey of parasitic diseases has revealed that one in every six people studied has one or more parasites living somewhere in his or her body.

—Ronald Kotulak

Parasites: An Epidemic in Disguise

A parasite epidemic in America? You must be joking! This is a clean, well-fed nation — parasites are only a serious problem in Third World countries . . . aren't they?

This attitude — that Americans are too clean, too civilized, too well-fed and too well-educated for parasites to be a serious problem — is surprisingly prevalent. Yet, there are about 300 types of parasites thriving in America today, including pinworms, tapeworms, hookworms, ringworms, whipworms, roundworms and *Giardia lamblia.* In fact, the microscopic parasite, Giardia, has infected the waterways in many of our nation's parks. Parasites know no national boundaries. They are oblivious to your income, your nationality, your age and your beliefs. More than 80% of the world's population is infected with parasites, which can range in size from microscopic to 20 feet in length. According to the Center for Disease Control, virtually every known parasitic disease has been diagnosed in the United States!

Most people know you can get tapeworms from eating under-cooked pork. But did you know you can get parasites from eating a rare steak? Or from just shaking hands with an infected person? Or from playing with your pet? You might even get parasites from your children — who picked up the little freeloaders from their friends at school. You can also get parasites from eating raw vegetables on which the tiny parasite eggs are laid. Sex also spreads parasites: they are more easily passed than venereal diseases through sexual practices.

The two major factors that make an epidemic of parasites possible are: 1) lack of sanitation, and 2) colons which are clogged and impacted from years of improper eating habits, providing a warm and well-fed breeding ground for worms and parasites to proliferate.

You may have very clean habits in your own kitchen, but do you eat out in restaurants? Many restaurants and food handlers are shockingly negligent in the most basic sanitation practices.

And how aware are you about the health of your intestinal tract? Parasites usually live in the intestinal tract, where they look forward to a steady diet of their favorite foods: sugar-laden desserts, and fried, processed and other junk foods. Even if you have a healthy, well-balanced diet, once your system is infected with parasites, you are at their mercy. They breed happily, growing fat and sassy stealing your nutrition, drinking your blood, and fouling your system with their wastes, which are reabsorbed into your bloodstream and carried to all parts of your body. Parasites take a heavy toll on the immune system and its function, causing many secondary health disorders such as allergies, bacterial infections, candida and mineral deficiences.

Symptoms of parasitic infestation run a wide range. Roundworms cause fever, cough and intestinal problems. Hookworms cause anemia, abdominal pain, diarrhea, apathy, malnutrition and even under-development in children. Whipworms cause abdominal pain and diarrhea.

The fecal matter from a single tapeworm can make humans ill. The worms may become so numerous as to cause intestinal obstruction as well as gas and intestinal distress. Tapeworm eggs in the liver can be mistaken for cancer and chemotherapy may be administered. The chemo will kill the eggs, but may also harm the patient.

Bloodflukes create lesions in the lungs and cause hemorrhages under the skin. They are often found in AIDS patients. Protozoa, such as amoeba, do not suck blood like the hookworm and others do, but these creatures cause arthritis-like pains or leukemia-like symptoms, and generally weaken the entire system.

Giardia lamblia, a protozoan parasite resembling the single-celled amoeba, is the most prevalent parasite in the U.S. today and is considered the number one cause of waterborne disease in the country. Giardia causes diarrhea, weakness, weight loss, abdominal cramps, nausea, belching and fever. The tiny parasites can coat the inside lining of the small intestine and prevent the lining from absorbing nutrients from food.

The multitude of different symptoms caused by parasites can be baffling to many doctors, who receive little training in diagnosing and treating parasitic infections. Unless people have major symptoms, doctors often misdiagnose cases as bacterial infections, but unfortunately, antibiotics have no effect on most parasites.

An effective herbal program as well as colon cleansing (colonics) can go a long way toward eliminating parasites and accumulated, impacted wastes in the large intestine. These wastes can be caused by eating the wrong kinds of foods, drinking too little liquid, lack of exercise, improper combination of foods, emotional distress, and weak muscle tone of the colon. Removal of these wastes by colon cleansing — wherein the colon is flushed with filtered water through a series of fills and releases — results in a renewed sense of health, vitality and energy in the individual's entire system.

But to remove all the parasites which may be living in the colon, small intestine, blood stream and many organs of the body it is essential to embark upon an effective parasite elimination program, in conjunction with colon cleansings.

Parasites can be destroyed harmlessly without injury to the body and without dangerous drugs by following one of the *Healing Within* 60-Day Parasite Elimination Programs. These programs start with the "parasite killer" colon complements: Gozarte with Neo-Pararte; or, for persons who also have a candida problem, Gozarte with Udarte. Pasaloc and Padapco are a good choice if the individual is taking a lot of anti-oxidants and can't reduce them for the 60-day period. Pasaloc and Padapco are also a good choice if worms are present. Finally, Biocidin, Biotonic, K-Min, Black Walnut Tincture, Castor Oil Capsules, *Healing Within* Intestinal Cleanser and Latero Flora are included in the programs. The immune system is strengthened by the use of Echinacea, Shitake Mushroom Capsules and DDS Acidophilus. Finally, the addition of Intestinalis Herbal Cleanser at the end of the *Healing Within* Parasite Elimination Program protects the intestinal tract from reinfestation. These products will destroy almost every parasite known to humankind.

Gozarte, Udarte, Neo-Pararte, Pasaloc, Padapco, Phyll Martin, Para-Citro, and **Mon Paradise** are powerful herbal combinations organically grown in the rain forests of Columbia. K-Min is a balance of mined elements that will, by ionization, rip worms apart. Since parasites rarely pass out of the body whole (and antibiotics have little effect on them), **K-Min** was devised to rip them up. **Black Walnut Tincture,** an herbal fluid, is very effective against parasites that may make their way into the bloodstream and to other organs of the body. In fact, K-Min and Black Walnut Tincture can be given to animals to rid them of parasites.

Good old-fashioned castor oil is not a mineral oil; it is the oil of the castor plant bean and for centuries has been known as a potent laxative. Castor oil lubricates the walls of the colon and helps loosen the hardened, impacted waste materials. Thanks to modern science, you can now take this cathartic and intestinal-wall lubricant without the unpleasant taste by ingesting frozen Castor Oil Capsules. The frozen capsules pass through the stomach and do not dissolve until they reach the small intestine, where they do the most good.

Healing Within **Intestinal Cleanser** contains gentian, golden seal, buckthorn, rhubarb root, cascara sagrada, and aloe vera, all well-calculated and delicately balanced in proportions essential for the success of the cleanser and detoxifier. This grouping pulls mucous, detoxifies, heals, acts as a diuretic, activates flushing of the liver and production of bile, and improves intestinal peristalsis.

Latero Flora *(Bacillus laterosporus* - B.O.D. Strain) normalizes the flora in the human digestive tract, aids in digestion and toxin elimination, and discourages the growth of yeast, fungi and other pathogenic micro-organisms. Latero Flora is extremely effective for individuals with gastro-intestinal disturbances, food allergies, and candidiasis hypersensitivity syndrome. No other product in existence is as effective as Latero Flora in restoring the original, desirable bacterial balance to the intestines, thus aiding in resolving many immuno-suppresses conditions.

Biocidin is a unique botanical formula manufactured with the finest pharmaceutical grade organically grown wildcrafted herbs and chlorophyll. Utilizing a unique extraction process, the cellular structure of the plant materials is broken down over the course of several months, insuring maximum bio-availability. No alchohol or solvents are used. Biocidin is considered by many health professionals to be the most effective formulation of its kind. It is known to have unusually broad spectrum activity against parasites.

Biotonic is based on two classical Chinese herbal combinations which have been utilized for centuries to balance digestive function and energy metabolism. Biotonic contains high quantities of Astragalus and includes Artemesia, Siberian Ginsing, as well as botanicals which aid in liver function and detoxification. Biotonic is specifically designed to balance the nature of Biocidin. Biotonic contains all natural herbal ingredients of the highest grade.

The *Healing Within* **Parasite Elimination Program** is a safe, non-toxic, natural and effective method of eliminating all types of parasites from the body. The combination of herbs provides the greatest strength and efficacy of any known parasite elimination products in the world. Where others have failed, these products have succeeded.

In conjunction with the program, it is also highly advisable to have professional colon cleansings once a week if available in your area* to assist in the removal of live and dead parasites and accumulated colon wastes. If colon cleansings are not available, several enemas a week are essential.

Completing the program will not necessarily be easy. Work and dedication are required, but the rewards may be greater than you can imagine. The results of a *Healing Within* Parasite Elimination Program and colon cleansings can include elimination of painful and uncomfortable symptoms, a stronger immune system, a greater sense of vitality and well-being, clearer thinking and improved memory, and an increased zest for life. Remember, the old adage, "Health, wealth and happiness" always begins with health!

Note: If you are not aware of the location of a colonic therapist in your area, call the following toll-free number. They may be able to assist you. Call 800-237-5911. Ask for Ray Dotolo.

Worms Outrank Cancer as Man's Deadliest Enemy

by Dolly Katz

Every year, the American Cancer Society publishes the names of famous people, such as Duke Ellington and Jack Benny, who have died of cancer. This is done, the society says, as "a dramatic reminder of the full dimensions of cancer's human devastation."

When Abdel Halim Hafez, the most popular singer in the Arab world, died last year, his name did not appear on any list, although the disease that killed him causes more human devastation than cancer does. Hafez, 46, died from complications of schistosomiasis, an infection of parasitic worms that live in the intestines. Worldwide, an estimated 200 million people — the equivalent of the entire U.S. population — are infected with this disease.

And the schistosomiasis worm is only one of many parasites, ranging in size from microscopic single-celled animals to foot-long roundworms, which annually kill many more people than cancer does. The diseases they cause are as well known as malaria and as obscure as kala-azar, which particularly affetcs children and is 90 percent fatal if untreated.

One of every four people in the world is infected by roundworms, which cause fever, cough, and intestinal problems. A quarter of the world's people have hookworms, which can cause anemia and abdominal pain. A third of a billion people suffer from the abdominal pain and diarrhea caused by whipworms.

Not much research is being done on these diseases. The U.S. spends more than $800 million a year on cancer research. All the nations of the world combined spend less than one-twentieth that amount studying parasitic diseases. As a result, there are no vaccines against them, and many of them are difficult or impossible to treat. There is no known treatment, for instance, for Chagas' disease, a variant of African sleeping sickness that occurs in South and Central America.

But while these diseases occur predominately in underdeveloped countries, the U.S. is not immune to them. Just about every parasitic disease known has been diagnosed in the U.S. in the last few years: schistosomiasis, trichinosis, giardiasis, toxoplasmosis, African sleeping sickness.

Most, like malaria, are imported cases brought back by travelers. But a significant number are entrenched in parts of our environment, kept alive in the U.S. by person-to-person transmission.

Pinworms, for example, parasites that live in the lower intestine and rectum, are the most common parasitic infection of children in temperate countries. At least one in five children in the general population has pinworms; in institutions, the figure can go as high as 90 percent.

All this doesn't mean that Americans ought to add parasites to the long list of diseases we're supposed to worry about when we develop symptoms. But it's interesting and perhaps important to realize that to most of the world's people, cancer is as exotic a disease as sleeping sickness is to us.

Reprinted from The Miami Herald, *June 25, 1978.*

Parasites More Common Than Believed, Study Says

by Ronald Kotulak

The first major nationwide survey of parasitic diseases has revealed that one in every six people studied has one or more parasites living somewhere in his or her body.

The prevalence of these parasitic stowaways, which range from microscopic organisms to 15-foot tapeworms, has come as a big surprise, especially to physicians who receive little training in diagnosing and treating parasitic infections.

"We think of this country as a highly sanitized country," Dr. Myron G. Schulz said, "but that is not necessarily true."

The large number of parasites, he said, means they are causing many diseases that baffle doctors.

"Many patients have experienced weeks of delay before the correct diagnosis was made and have been subjected to unnecessary laboratory tests, hospitalization, and even surgery," Shultz, director of the parasitic diseases division of the Centers for Disease Control (CDC) in Atlanta, warned in an editorial appearing in an upcoming issue of the Journal of the American Medical Association.

He said that the presence of parasites also means that many Americans are not as "clean" as they thought they were.

"What concerns me is that somewhere along the line there has been a breakdown in sanitation measures and people have ingested contaminated food, water, or dirt," said Dr. Dennis Juranek, assistant chief of the CDC's parasitic diseases division.

9

The survey pinpointed four problems:

- A parasite that causes intestinal infections is sweeping across the country. Called *Giardia lamblia*, the parasite has now become the number one cause of waterborne disease in the nation.

- Tapeworm infections appear to have increased by 100 percent in the last ten years, an increase that may be linked to American's increasing fondness for raw or rare beef.

- Amebiasis, the most deadly of the parasites, continues to be a serious problem, with recent outbreaks in South Carolina. Between 1969 and 1973 there were 242 reported deaths from amebiasis, a microscopic organism usually passed from person to person.

- Illinois farmers are being plagued by a Balatidium parasite from pigs that causes intestinal infections in humans.

The survey involved examinations of 414,820 samples of feces in 1976. The examinations were performed by 570 public and private laboratories in all 50 states and the results sent to the CDC.

According to the survey, 15.6 percent of the specimens contained one or more parasites. About half these parasites are capable of causing disease.

The large number of parasitic infections discovered in the survey may not reflect the actual rate of infection in the general public, but it does reveal that the problem is much more widespread than most health professionals thought.

"I'm sure that this high infection rate comes as a surprise to those who never considered parasitic diseases to be a major problem in the U.S.," Dr. Juranek said.

The biggest problem uncovered in the survey was the high rate of infection with the Giardia parasite.

This parasite now appears to have spread to almost every state and is responsible for recend epidemics in upstate New York, Colorado, Washington, New Hampshire and Wisconsin.

This bug, a protozoan parasite, is microscopic in size and resembles a single-celled amoeba. The parasite coats the inside lining of the small intestine and prevents the lining from absorbing nutrients from food.

Although not a killer, it causes illness characterized by diarrhea, weakness, weight loss, abdominal cramps, nausea, vomiting, belching, and fever.

Most cases are misdiagnosed as bacterial infections, but unfortunately antibiotics have little effect on the parasite, Dr. Juranek said. Two drugs are effective in curing Giardias: atabrine, an antimalarial agent, and metronidazole.

Hundreds of small water systems throughout the country that do not adequately purify water may be contaminated with the parasite, said Dr. John Hoff, an EPA research microbiologist.

Streams or watersheds may become contaminated through infected human sewage, and recent studies show that Giardia-infected beavers may also contaminate water sources.

Reprinted from The Chicago Tribune Service.

Parasites and AIDS

by Rev. Hanna Kroeger

AIDS (Acquired Immune Deficiency Syndrome) is not one disease in itself. Rather it is caused by the accumulation of several factors that weaken the immune system so drastically that the body is susceptible to many other diseases.

Parasites, such as hookworm and protozoa, are found in almost all carriers of AIDS. The most common type of hookworm found, *Hydatoxi lualba,* is microscopic and can travel into the lung tissue making lesions. It also can be found in the brain, intestines, rectum, and intracutaneous tissue. It is the same microscopic disturbance that causes uremic poisoning during pregnancy.

Widespread protozoa, a freshwater parasite causing weakening of the entire system, is also found in AIDS carriers. Protozoa do not suck blood as the hookworm does, but that make arthritis-like pains, leukemia symptoms, bleeding under the skin, and a host of other symptoms. Dr. Bingham, author of the book *Fight Back Against Arthritis,* states on page 52:

> *Overall, it seems highly probable that various species of free-living protozoa are the etiological agent of collagene-anti-immune disease which show every graduation and combination with one another. They are not due to a single organism, but to a number of similar organisms. Such a parasitic infection would explain the urticaria asthma and easinophilia observed in many cases of collagene or auto-immune diseases.*

Sometimes flukes and flatworms are found in the blood of AIDS sufferers. These bloodflukes make lesions in the lungs and hemorrhages under the skin.

Finally, *Candida albicans*, the hidden epidemic, is always found in AIDS victims. This fungus overgrowth can affect every organ and part of the body and is the worst of the fungi that attack the nervous system.

Reprinted by permission of Rev. Hanna Kroeger, 7075 Valmont Drive, Boulder, CO 80301.

Note: Although Dr. Louis Parrish reports only some success with his method of treatment in the following article, the *Healing Within* Herbal Parasite Elimination Program has a high success rate. Rarely does the herbal program have to be repeated, unless there is a reinfestation of parasites. Preventing a parasitic infestation is now possible thanks to a new herbal combination from Colombia called Consolar. Consolar sets up a barrier in the stomach against parasites and should be taken before eating meals in restaurants or when traveling. Refer to page 71 to order.   — S.W.

The Protozoal Syndrome

by Louis Parrish, M.D.

For almost two decades, I have been trying to raise medical and lay community awareness regarding a major health problem, infections of intestinal protozoa *Entamoeba histolytica* and *Giardia lamblia*, which alone or together are often devastating to the quality of a person's life. Although separate diseases, they have so much in common that I refer to them collectively as The Protozoal Syndrome.

The symptoms these organisms produce in humans are so varied, intermittent and similar to other infections involving the immune system, that only relatively recently are they being recognized as a primary cause of generalized illness.

A Brief History

Intestinal parasite have existed since our evolution as homo sapiens, yet were only recognized as medical entities in the last 200 years. These protozoa may even have been a factor in

Darwinian selection. Diarrheal diseases are a primary cause of infant mortality. Those with a strong immune system and better nutrition survive, but during their lives many may never recognize a normal bowel or realize their full energy potential. I have often wondered if the Latin siesta was not a cultural manifestation of unnatural lethargy caused by these organisms.

These prevalent, potentially disabling diseases, especially amoebic dysentery, became important diagnoses along with typhoid fever in the early 1900s. With the New Deal, work forces did a laudable job cleaning up the environment, setting standards to eliminate polluted water and establishing public health centers. The incidence of Amoebiasis and Giardiasis was reduced during that time period, though never controlled. In the last five decades they have been on the rise due to world wars, peripedantic tourists, and most importantly, immigrant food handlers from endemic areas.

Millions Affected in USA Alone

Based on my experience, I estimate in the New York metropolitan area that 25 percent of the population is infected. Of these, 15 percent are asymptomatic, 25 percent have ignorable symptoms, 55 percent have a compromised quality of life, and 5 percent are disabled. Using a conversion factor of .1 among 300 million U.S. inhabitants, I feel confident in estimating that 7 million people are infected. In addition, virtually every sexually transmitted AIDS patient I have seen is, or has been, infected with Amoebiasis or Giardiasis.

Effects on the Immune System

A Giardia invasion of the duodenum and upper small intestine can significantly reduce production of Immunoglobulin A, the most important source of secretory antibodies. Furthermore, in relating an endemic outbreak of Amoebiasis two years prior to the outbreak of AIDS in San Francisco, researchers from the University of Virginia reported that amoebas can project an activated substance, a lectin, which ruptures the immune defense cells that have by ingestion inactivated the HIV virus. Freed into the bloodstream, they multiply and manifest their lethal potential. The implications of an amoebic infection on immune function are obvious and applicable to other viral infections.

Alarming Misconceptions

The medical establishment rests shamefully complacent with some alarming misconceptions about these diseases:

Misconception 1: These diseases exist only in tropical, unsanitary geographic areas.

• The fact is that there are other areas where the infections are alarmingly prevalent, with the U.S.A. having a high but unrecognized incidence. These pathogenic organisms thrive in areas as diverse as the cold rushing mountain streams and placid lakes of our national parks, which beavers and perhaps other animals have contaminated with their feces, to the sushi and salad bars of our metropolitan areas, transmitted by "fecal fingers" of food handlers, especially immigrants from countries where hand washing is not routine after a bowel evacuation.

• Recently at a large Manhattan hotel I asked the attendant in the men's room to count the number of people who entered the stalls and how many washed their hands when they came out. In a two-hour period 112 entered, but only 60 washed their hands. Assuming that 15 percent of those only urinated and were less likely to wash, 44 could have left with potentially contaminated hands. The bathroom was located at the site of Health Convention! This anecdotal report reflects the insidious spread of these infections.

Misconception 2: These diseases are species specific, passed only from human to human.

• There is increasing evidence to challenge this assumption. Besides the wild animals that pollute the outdoor water supplies, pooper-scoopers, cat litter attendants, as well as parakeet owners, are all at risk of contracting the disease from their pets.

Misconception 3: An accurate diagnosis can be obtained from a single stool exam.

• Good parasitology teaches that one must get three specimens. If they are negative and one is still clinically suspicious, get three to six more. Some authorities recommend treating all patients with a suggestive clinical presentation, even if no protozoa are found. Often a therapeutic trial is the best diagnostic procedure.

Misconception 4: Treatment with a single course of metronizadole-Flagyl is 90 percent effective.

• Fact: 25 years ago this may have been true. But the protozoa rapidly became resistant. Today the single course cure rate is less than 5 percent. Furthermore, approximately half of the patients treated with metronizadole complain of side effects, and 10 percent flatly refuse to take it ever again.

Symptoms

After 30 years' experience, I have divided the many symptoms of The Protozoal Syndrome into three categories:

Gastrointestinal: Oral thrush, indigestion, acid reflux, epigastric discomfort, malabsorption, gas, foul flatus, mucus sometimes blood-tinged, erratic and unpredictable bowel movements, urgency, weird stool formations — from explosive liquid diarrhea to prolonged periods of constipation and anal irritation.

Fatigue: Persistent tiredness, excessive yet unrefreshing sleep, lack of motivation, "brownouts" — a need to nap at any cost.

Toxicity: A constant feeling of being sick or unwell, hypothetically one of the results of the production and release by the protozoa of a substance which disorders the normal function of some organ or system. It may result in lack of concentration,

17

confused memory, impaired motivation, nightmares, musculoskeletal pains, wide swings in blood sugar levels and menstrual irregularities.

In all cases, the severity of symptoms depends on a person's natural resistance, the amount of innoculum, secondary bacterial infections, and the host's nutritional status. It is interesting to note that these symptoms also appear in many of today's controversial diagnoses, such as Candidiasis, Epstein-Barr Virus and CMV. Frequently these diagnoses are made out of frustration. The practitioner does not have a clear clinical picture and can't get any positive procedural or lab results to be more specific.

The poor response of some of these patients may be due to a protozoal infection that has been missed or inadequately treated. I have successfully treated a significant number of patients with chronic candidiasis by controlling the protozoal infection. Restoring the integrity of the intestinal mucosa removes the unhealthy and fertile environment for yeast growth. I have also had success with patients with the "trashbasket diagnoses" of irritable bowel syndrome (IBS) and chronic fatigue syndrome (CFS).

These diagnoses inherently imply an emotional etiology when 15 percent, conservatively estimated, have a treatable protozoal infection. These patients' protracted unwellness is due in part to the lack of their practitioners' awareness of the prevalence of these diseases and in part to their too easy acceptance of negative stool reports for ova and parasites.

Proper Diagnostic Use of the Rectal Swab Technique (RST)

The proper method of diagnosing these diseases is first getting a pertinent clinical history, with emphasis on date of onset of symptoms, in relation to the patient's travel or residential history. Lab reports are critical for a practitioner inexperienced in this field. Unfortunately, these reports are notoriously false negative for several reasons. The specimen is fecal matter which represents only the contents of the bowel lumen; the specimen is not fresh; and the technician is not adequately trained.

Before they closed in the 1980s due to New York's financial crisis, the public health tropical disease labs were very accurate. After that, several Manhattan labs specialized in parasitological diseases and did purge stool exams. Although these are much better specimens and a certain percent of false negatives are to be expected, I was dissatisfied, particularly in my own case, with repeated negative reports when clinically I knew I was infected.

By necessity I initiated the rectal swab technique (RST), which is basically a superficial biopsy and discovered the protozoa myself in my own sample. The RST is far more accurate than casual stool exams and at least 25 percent more accurate and more practical than purged stool exams. Another benefit is the use of the anoscope, which allows examination of mucosal integrity. With an experienced technician immediately at hand, the results and treatment, if necessary, can be discussed in a single office visit.

Treatment

Success in treating these parasitic infections depends on a variety of factors, including length of time of infection, natural resistance, patient cooperation, repeated exposures, etc. My clinical impression is that the length of time needed to obtain a "satisfactory" result is related conceptually to the time the patient has been infected and gone untreated. In most cases I have treated, repeated courses are necessary just to establish control.

"Satisfactory" results are often the removal or reduction of severity of the symptoms, so that the patient is able to lead a life with acceptable bowel habits and normal energy. This does not mean that the parasites have been totally eliminated, which I have found is accomplished in only about 20 to 40 percent of the cases, an efficacy reflecting the length of an infestation before therapeutic intervention.

Medicines Available

I do not think one medicine is superior, but efficacy is dependent on consecutive on-going courses of different protozides and combinations. The medication, dosage and length of a course of treatment must all be individualized to the patient's tolerance of the drugs and his or her lifestyle. The management of cases varies and frequently evokes a practitioner's creativity. Medicines for Amoebiasis are idoquinol, paramomycin-Humatin and the tetracyclines.

Lilly recently ceased marketing the arsenical Carbarsonc, because they "didn't feel there was a need for an amoebicide." For Giardiasis there are quinacrine-Atabrine and furazolidone-Furozone. For both there is metronizadole-Flagyl. I do not feel it is essential for the successful treatment of The Protozoal Syndrome, but if tolerated it should be included as a single or repeated course in a therapeutic regimen.

My patients have taught me that the end-point of therapy is not a negative lab report, but an improvement in or restoration of their quality of life. I have found that in a majority of improved cases, the lab reports may still be positive for protozoa, but the patient feels well. What appears to occur is that, with treatment, the protozoa are integrated into the several hundred other organism alive in a natural flora of the intestinal tract. There is still a possibility that stress will bring a recurrence, but then therapy can be resumed, along with emphasis on rebuilding the immune system once again.

Counseling Patients on Prevention

Treatment should be accompanied by counseling against reinfection, including advice to avoid salads and uncooked dishes such as sushi or fresh fruit compotes when dining out, drinking only bottled beverages and foregoing scatological sexual practices. People travelling abroad or in our national parks and wilderness areas should also boil or microfilter any non-bottled drinking water, or use several drops of an oxygenating liquid such as Acrox, which has been reported to kill the organisms through the addition of oxygen to the water, and also to take preventive medications.

Conclusions

Amoebiasis and Giardiasis are only recently being recognized as a forgotten cause of long-term illness in millions of Americans. The allopathic medical community has by undefinable social and scientific attitudes perfunctorily rejected these illnesses and too frequently accepted false negative lab results as fact.

The wide variety of gastrointestinal symptoms, fatigue and general toxicity can compromise a clinical picture and make these infections hard to diagnose.

The few drugs available to treat protozoal infections can have intolerable side effects and often do not eradicate the pathogens.

Millions are suffering from the symptoms of The Protozoal Syndrome and even after medical evaluations, are unaware of the real cause of their problem — the protozoa. Once diagnosed and properly treated, most can be restored to health.

Reprinted by permission of The Nutrition & Dietary Consultant, *March 1991.*

Danger in Diaperland: Giardia Linked to Day-Care Centers

by Penny Ward Moser

Late one night in July several years ago, I was talking on the phone to my mother. "How's Becky doing?" I asked of my sister, who'd been mysteriously ill for several months.

"You know," my mom said, "I'm really afraid she is going to die."

My mind froze. "Going to die?"

"Yes," my mother said. "She looks like a skeleton. She can barely get out of bed. And the doctors can't find anything wrong with her. They say it's just stress."

Just stress? My pretty, athletic, 29-year-old sister had in six months lost 25 pounds — 15 in June alone. She had relentless stomach problems, painful bloating and diarrhea. Ever a cheerleader, she was now deeply depressed and cried all the time. She had seen three doctors and gone to two hospitals for batteries of sometimes agonizing tests. Each time, she was told to slow down, take a look at her life and relax.

And now my mother thought we were loosing her.

The next afternoon, watching a ball game with friends, I kept thinking about my sister. Then I remembered that one of the men in the room had once had some strange intestinal disease.

A woman in my office had once mentioned giardia — a parasite, a tiny protozoa that looks like a cross-eyed tennis racket. I remembered she'd been sick for months. "My brains were fried," she told me. "I found myself sitting on the back steps at 2 in the morning, crying my eyes out." She then sang praises of Martin Wolfe, a tropical medicine specialist.

That night, I called my sister in Illinois and told her that she had to get on a plane the next day. Wolfe would see her immediately. But the next morning my sister collapsed in the hall outside her bedroom and was taken to the hospital.

"I'll tell you what we'll do," said Wolfe when I called. "Come over to the lab for some stool spectrum kits. Let's see if we can do this via Federal Express."

And so, every other day for a week, my sister sent specimens. In the meantime, I gave the doctor her case history. Becky had traveled to Mexico and to an area of the Colorado Rockies where there's giardia in the water. Her symptoms came and went, but each time they came on, they were worse. And she had developed a violent reaction to milk products.

One evening about a week later, Wolfe called me back. "I can't find giardia in your sister," he said. "But we don't always find it in three specimens. I did find evidence her intestinal immune system is fighting a parasite. Given the symptoms, history and the lactose intolerance, it sounds like giardia."

"I don't know what's going on out there," says Wolfe, "but since the 1970s I've just been seeing more and more giardiasis — many sad and tragic cases. People who have had physical after physical and thousands of dollars in tests, and all they have wrong is giardiasis."

Incredibly, no one, not even the Centers for Disease Control in Atlanta, actually knows what is going on out there. In 1984, just when giardia cases were exploding, the CDC (in a series of cutbacks) stopped keeping track nationwide. It did manage to note a record 26,560 cases that year, nearly double the number of cases a few years earlier.

But that's just the tip of a colossal iceberg. Scattered reports from the states paint a dismaying picture. Pennsylvania leads the nation in the number of water borne disease outbreaks — almost all from giardia — with 15,508 giardia cases reported from 1979 through 1990. Over the past eight years some 250,000 Pennsylvania residents have had to boil their drinking water, largely because of giardia contamination.

In New York state the number of reported cases of giardiasis jumped to 2,553 last year, up from 961 in 1986. Wisconsin had 1,911 cases last year, up from 118 in 1981. Washington state had 796, more than ten times the 75 they first counted in 1974. In Vermont, giardiasis is now the No. 1 reported disease.

And it's not just up in the hills somewhere. New York City is about to spend several billion dollars to filter the little critter out of its water supply.

So what is going on? For years, giardiasis was most often associated with travel — to Latin America, or Africa, or the Soviet Union. (Leningrad visitors regularly came home with "the Trotskys.") In this country, it was something that back-packers and hunters picked up by dipping their canteens in the wrong creek. Tainted stream water was so often linked to beavers that giardiasis got the nickname "beaver fever."

But as Wolfe puts it, "There just isn't enough beaver poop out there to be causing all of this." Almost everyone in the field now believes that we're getting giardia from each other. (In fact, we probably gave it to the beavers.) And contaminated water is only part of the picture.

When 16 people got sick from a noodle salad served at a Connecticut picnic in 1985, the CDC tracked the infection to a woman who had mixed the cold salad with her hands. She didn't have giardia, but one of her small children did — though without any symptoms. The woman had apparently helped the child with hygiene and gone directly back to work in the kitchen. Perhaps she thought her hands were clean. But with giardia, just 10 or a 100 organisms can zap you. A hundred would barely make a smudge under your fingernail. A soiled diaper might harbor millions.

That's why, when an infected New Jersey child recently had what the CDC describes as a "fecal accident" in a 175,000-gallon swimming pool, nine swimmers from the ladie's lap group that followed came down with the disease. Likewise, an "adopted grandparent" program in a Minnesota nursing home last year sent giardia pingponging from toddlers to food handlers to the elderly, laying low 88 people in six weeks.

The most alarming statistics, however, come from the nation's day-care centers. A recent CDC survey of day-care centers in Fulton County, Georgia, showed that a fourth of the kids are infected. In New Haven the rate has run as high as 50 percent. A report from the 1980s on 30 Houston centers chosen at random found at least one giardia-infected child in more than two-thirds of the centers. In one 10-year span, an Anaheim (Orange Country) day-care center saw the rate of toddler giardia infections jump from 3 to 43 percent. It's the same all over.

"Day-care centers are the open sewers of the 20th century." says a federal epidemiologist who specializes in intestinal illness. Sure enough, in an outbreak a few years ago at a day nursery in Toronto, when a fifth of the kids came down with the bug, their darling diapered bottoms carried it back to one of every four people they came in contact with at home.

And home is where the sufferers fall back, languishing on the couch, hovering near the bathroom, wondering why their doctor can't figure out what's wrong.

If the giardia parasites made themselves apparent, as, say, streptococcus bacteria do in strep throat, they wouldn't be such a problem. But giardia infections, while certainly detectable, are much trickier. A good infection can leave millions of tiny protozoa stuck tight to the intestinal lining. There, they cripple the gut's ability to secrete enzymes and absorb food. The distressing symptoms typically mimic bacterial food poisoning — but don't usually show up for nine or even 15 days. They can vanish, suddenly, then reappear. They may hide for months.

Adding to the confusion, says Wolfe, is the fact that many otherwise well-educated American doctors don't even know about the problem. "In the '50s and '60s, giardia was not generally considered something that could cause serious illness. And parasitology isn't even taught in some medical schools today."

A truly foolproof test would be a godsend for many victims. Sometimes the only symptom is a painful arthritis. Some patients complain of muscle weakness. Others develop severely itchy skin and mucous membranes. And in some people, giardia may kick up something similar to an allergic or immune system reaction. A Washington, D.C., study a few years back showed that patients with chronic giardiasis suffered more allergies than other patients did.

The frightening mood slumps are not well understood. New York internist Leo Galland believes the immune system's response to the parasite may trigger depression, as can deficiencies of the nutrient folic acid brought on by chronic diarrhea.

With so many uncertainties, giardiasis remains a disease of "somes." Some infections mysteriously vanish with no treatment at all. Some people become asymptomatic carriers. Some evidence suggests some people acquire a natural immunity to some strains. And some strains seem more virulent than others. This means that while you may be immune to a strain in Costa Rice, a drink from a stream on a California mountainside will nail you.

But no one can merely put the blame on mountain streams anymore. The fact is, many of our water treatment plants are not up to snuff. The outdated filters on some 3,000 U.S. water systems supplying 20 million people let giardia parasites pass right on through. And the bugs aren't necessarily fazed by the usual chlorine treatment that kills bacteria and viruses.

In a move prompted largely by giardiasis outbreaks, the Environmental Protection Agency has set forth new quality rules for all tap water systems that draw from rivers or lakes — including New York, Chicago, Los Angeles, San Francisco and scores of other cities and towns. If they can't prove their water is pure enough, they must either dig wells, install better filters or disinfection systems or hook up to neighboring systems that are already purified. The new filters must catch 99.9 percent of giardia, and must be in place by 1993.

Granted, cleaning up the nation's water systems won't stop the rampant infections at day-care centers, but it will help. Education and better hygiene will have to do the rest: Wash your hands top and bottom with soap and water after changing a child's diaper or playing with a puppy. *Pets can carry a strain of giardia that infects humans, though no one really knows how often this happens. Keep a nail brush by the sink, particularly if you work around children (who may carry the bug), or food (which can transmit it), or the elderly (whose frail immune systems leave them uncommonly vulnerable).*

Excerpted from *In Health* magazine ©1991.

A Brief Update of the Current Global Parasitic Epidemic

Geography and under-development are no longer the only criteria accounting for parasitic infestation. The most updated evaluations indicate that over 600 million people world-wide are infected with Amoebiasis, 300 million with Giardiasis, and over 100 million with Dientamoebiasis. A conservative estimate of the continental United States infection rate is 60% (30% Amoebiasis, 20% Giardiasis and 10% Dientamoebiasis). Contributing factors are local water supplies, the third world influx into major cosmopolitan areas, and travel abroad.

If you have ever been ill while on a foreign vacation and suffered the symptoms of parasite infestation, including diarrhea, nausea, fatigue and other symptoms, there is a good possibility that *you may still have a parasite problem, even though the symptoms may have disappeared.*

A Perspective of Modern Anti-Pathogenic Therapeutic Modalities

Recently, due to an outbreak of a very malignant chloroquine resistant malaria, the investigators of the World Health Organization have been instituting therapy with *Artemesia annua* (Vera), achieving surprising and dramatic results.

Because of these positive results, many authorities in the field are currently endeavoring to isolate the active agents responsible for this malaricidal effect. So far over 500 different chemical compounds have been isolated from this natural herb, many of them with anti-parasitic activity.

Instituting a great deal of this research, Dr. Herman Bueno has achieved many scientific breakthroughs and discoveries. He has pioneered the use of *Artemesia* and other equally effective but less well-known herbs for a variety of modalities, which are discussed in the following pages.

Parasitic Disease Incidences Worldwide

from *GEO Magazine*, June 1984

Disease	Symptoms	People Infected	People with Symptoms	Deaths per Year
Roundworm	Intestinal obstruction	1,000,000,000	1,000,000	20,000
Hookworm	Anemia	900,000,000	1,500,000	50,000
Malaria	Fever, coma	800,000,000	150,000,000	1,200,000
Trichuriasis	Intestinal disease	500,000,000	10,000	Low
Amoebiasis	Dysentary	400,000,000	1,500,000	30,000
Filariasis	Elephantiasis	250,000,000	3,000,000	Low
Giardiasis	Diarrhea	200,000,000	500,000	Very Low
Bilharziasis	Liver/urinary fibrosis	200,000,000	20,000,000	750,000
Onchocerciasis	Blindness	30,000,000	500,000	35,000
Trypanosomiasis:				
South American	Heart disease	12,000,000	1,200,000	60,000
African	Sleeping sickness	1,000,000	10,000	5,000
Leishmanjasis	Sores, fever, anemia	12,000,000	12,000,000	5,000

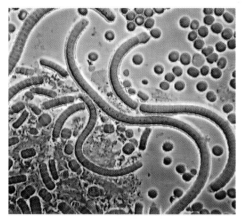

parasitic annelids
Courtesy American Biologics

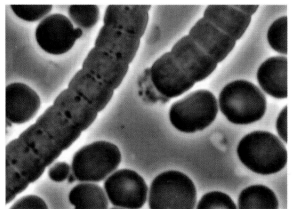

parasitic annelids
Courtesy American Biologics

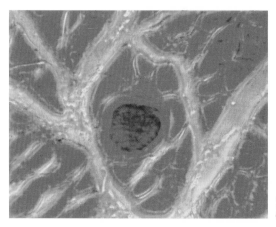

Trichinella spiralis
Courtesy American Biologics

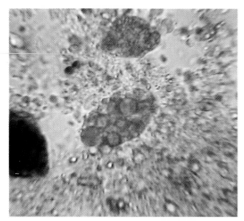

Ascaris lumbricoides
Courtesy Institute of Parasitic Diseases

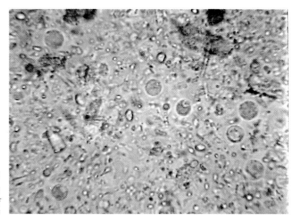

Blastocystis hominis
Courtesy Institute of Parasitic Diseases

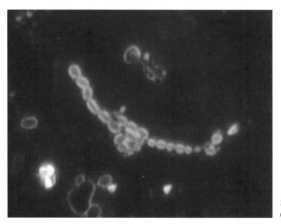

unidentified
Courtesy American Biologics

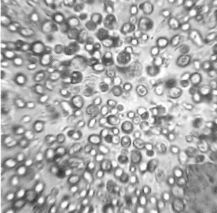

Candida albicans
Courtesy Institute of Parasitic Diseases

Charcot-Leyden Crystals
Courtesy Institute of Parasitic Diseases

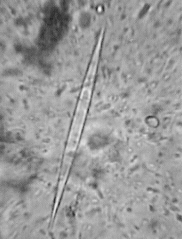

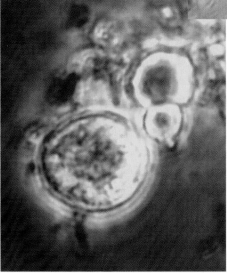

Entamoeba Coli
Courtesy American Biologics

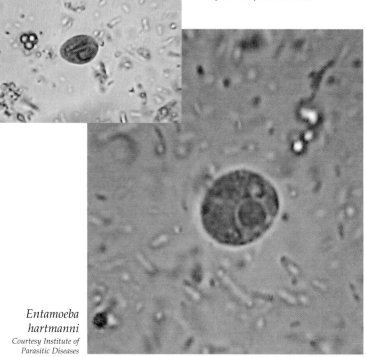

Giardia lamblia
Courtesy Institute of Parasitic Diseases

Entamoeba
hartmanni
Courtesy Institute of
Parasitic Diseases

Entamoeba hartmanni Courtesy Institute of Parasitic Diseases

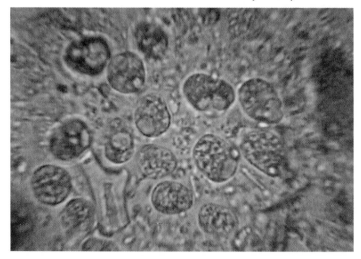

Parasite Questionnaire

1. Have you ever developed diarrhea or abdominal distress while visiting a foreign country or another part of the U.S.?   Yes ___ No ___

2. Is the consistency of your bowel movement changeable — some–times hard and then soft for no apparent reason?   Yes ___ No ___

3. Do you have unexplained periods of indigestion?   Yes ___ No ___

4. Do you frequently feel bloated or gaseous for no apparent reason in the area of the navel or below?   Yes ___ No ___

5. Does your intestinal tract burn, cramp or feel irritable for no apparent reason?   Yes ___ No ___

6. Do you have periods of fatigue for no apparent reason?   Yes ___ No ___

7. Do you develop frequent colds, flu or other acute illnesses?   Yes ___ No ___

8. Have you developed allergies to foods and environment in recent years?   Yes ___ No ___

9. Do you have a recurring feeling of unwellness?   Yes ___ No ___

10. Do you have a recurring candida overgrowth problem?   Yes ___ No ___

If you answered yes to 5 or more of these questions, you may want to have your doctor order a laboratory test for parasites. *Even though the test may come back negative, there is still a strong possibility that parasites may be present.*

Laboratory Description of Common Parasites

Giardia lamblia: *Giardia* is a pathogenic lumen dwelling protozoa which parasitizes the upper intestinal tract. The trophozoite is the active parasitic form, but often only the cysts appear in the rectum. *Giardia* may cause gastrointestinal disturbances, food intolerances, fatigue, immunologic dysfunction and malabsorption. Treatment of giardiasis is recommended even in asymptomatic individuals because of the risk of activation and spread.

Entamoeba histolytica: This organism parasitizes the human large intestine and may cause bowel disturbances, food intolerance, fatigue and immunologic dysfunction. Pathogenicity depends upon the strain of amoeba. Migration of the organism to the liver and brain may occur concomitant with very heavy infestation of especially invasive strains.

Entamoeba hartmanni: Formerly called the "small race" of *E. histolytica,* the pathogenicity of this organism falls into a grey area of some dispute. As for histolytica, pathogenicity may relate to the specific strain.

Cryptosporidium: This is a minute coccidian parasite with worldwide distribution. It parasitizes the entire small and large intestine. In immunocompetent patients, symptomatic cryptosporidiosis generally produces a self-limited diarrhea and occasionally abdominal discomfort, anorexia, fever, nausea and weight loss. In immunodeficient patients, severe diarrhea and systemic symptoms are typical and the organism has been associated with malabsorption and hematogenous spread. The usual antiparasitic drugs are ineffective against cryptosporidiosis. In 1993, 430,000 people in Milwaukee fell ill from this protozoa. More than 125 died and many remain ill. This outbreak took place because the water district's usual method of filtration and chemicals used to kill bacteria and parasites does not effectively kill cryptosporidium. As of this date, none of the water districts across the U.S. have an effective method of eliminating this parasite from drinking water. For this reason you are urged to not drink tap water that is not properly filtered. An outbreak can happen anywhere.

Blastocystis hominis: The taxonomic status of this organism is unclear. Its pathogenicity appears to be low, although it has been implicated as a cause of chronic diarrhea in travellers. Blastocystis may not require treatment unless the infestation is heavy and gastrointestinal or immunologic dysfunction is evident.

Endolimax nana: This is a common lumen dwelling protozoa which has generally been considered non-pathogenic. Reactive arthritis provoked by *Endolimax* infection has been reported, so that treatment is warranted in individuals with active inflammatory disorders.

Entamoeba coli: This is a common non-pathogenic protozoan. Its presence in the rectal swab indicates exposure to food or water contaminated with feces, but is not, in itself, an indication for treatment.

Iodamoeba butschli: This uncommon amoeba is generally non-pathogenic and treatment is usually not warranted.

Trichomonas hominis: The presence of this organism is indicative of direct fecal contamination, but there is no evidence it plays a pathogenic role in humans.

Dientamoeba fragilis: This organism may be pathogenic, causing bowel disturbances and immunologic dysfunction. Treatment of *Dientamoeba fragilis* is generally indicated.

33

Yeasts: Most yeasts found in the intestinal mucosa are described as dimorphic, in that they can exist in two states: the vegetative state usually referred to as hyphal, and the budding form where individual cells replicate by mitotic budding. The hyphal form is usually considered pathogenic, whereas the presence of a small number of budding yeasts is probably normal. Following is a glossary of frequently used terms:

Blastoconidium: A conidium formed by budding along a hypha, pseudohypha, or single cell, as in the yeasts.

Chlamydoconidium: A conidium that is thick walled and contains stored food. It may be located at the end of the hypha (terminally) or inserted along the hypha, singly or in *chains*.

Chlamydospore: A thick-walled vesicle formed by *Candida albicans.* It neither germinates nor produces conidia when mature.

Conidium (pl. conidia): Asexual propagule that forms on the side or end of the hypha or conidiophore. It may consist of one or more cells, and the size, shape and arrangement in groups are generally characteristic of the organism.

Hypha (pl. hyphae): A tubular or threadlike structure of a fungus. Many together form a mycelium.

Mycelium (pl. mycelia): A mat or intertwined hyphae that constitutes the colony of a fungus.

Pseudohyphae: Chains of cells formed by budding that, when elongated, resemble true hyphae. They differ from true hyphae by being constricted at the septa, forming branches that begin with septation and having terminal cells smaller than the other cells.

Common Parasitic Diseases

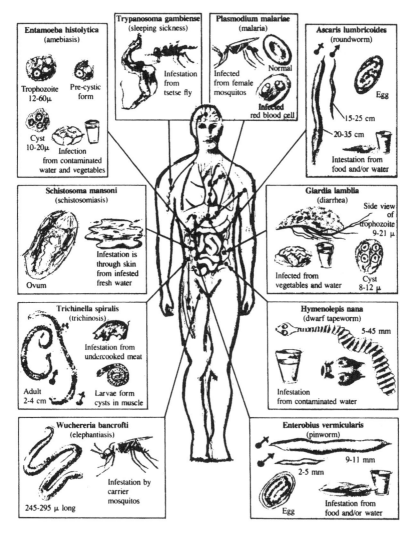

The above diagram illustrates ten common parasites, their source, and the areas of the body they are most likely to affect. Contaminated water is the most common breeding ground for parasites, and many water supplies in the U.S.A. are known to contain *Giardia lamblia*. Whenever possible, drink purified water. Avoid drinking river and stream water unless it is properly treated.

A New Generation of Herbal Parasite Fighters Has Arrived!

Presenting . . . The Healing Within Parasite Elimination Program

The *Healing Within* Parasite Elimination Program consists of three groups of powerful herbal products and regular colon cleansings:

- The Colon Complements: Biocidin, Biotonic, Para-Citro, Mon Paradise, Phyll-Martin, Gozarte, Udarte, Neo-Pararte, Pasaloc, Padapco, K-Min, Black Walnut Tincture, Castor Oil Capsules, Intestinal Cleanser and Latero Flora
- Immune System Strengtheners: Echinacea, Shitake Mushroom Capsules and DDS Acidophilus
- Post-Program Maintenance: Intestinalis Herbal Cleanser
- Colon Cleansings: Colonic irrigation and enemas hasten expulsion of waste. Try to have a colonic once a week during the program to flush out parasites and other toxins. If colonics are not available in your area, give yourself a home enema twice a week.

The Colon Complements

All eight herbal combinations — Gozarte, Udarte, Mon Paradise, Neo-Pararte, Para-Citro, Pasaloc, Padapco, and Phyll-Martin — are the highest quality and most potent herbs available for parasite elimination. The herbs are organically grown in the tropical rain forests of Columbia without the use of pesticides or chemical fertilizers. These safe, effective and non-toxic therapeutic herbal agents have been produced after many years of research by Herman Bueno, M.D., PhD., a renowned parasitologist and member of the American Society of Tropical Medicine and Hygiene.

Some of the Organisms Affected by Gozarte, Para-Citro, Phyll-Martin, Mon Paradise, Udarte, Neo-Pararte, Pasaloc and Padapco

Gozarte, Para-Citro, Phyll-Martin, Mon Paradise, Udarte, Neo-Pararte, Pasaloc and Padapco have an extremely broad spectrum of activity. The following is a list of some affected organisms:

Entamoeba histolytica	*Dientamoeba fragiles*
Giardia lamblia	Causitive organisms for malaria
Blastocystis hominus	Schistosoma
Nematodes	*Oxuilus vermicularis*
Alcaligones faecalis	*Enterobacter eloacae*
Pseudomonas aeruginosa	*Flavobacterium* spp.
Micrococcus spp.	*Alpha streptococci*
Streptococcus pyogones	*Chaetomium elatum*
Salmonella typhosa	*Bacillus subtillus*
Brucella arbortus	*Aspergillus niger*
Pullularia pullulans	*Staphylococcus aureus*
Staphylococcus pyogenes	*Staphylococcus saprophyticus*
Staphylococcus faecalies	*Bacillus subtilis*
Bacillus mycoides	*Cryptosporidium*

Gram-Negative Bacteria

Proteus mirabilis	*Proteus vulgaris*
Escherichia coli	*Salmonella anatum*
Salmonella choleraesuis	*Salmonella typhi*
Salmonella paratyphi	*Salmonella schorttmuelleri*
Shigella dysenteriae	*Pseudomonas aeruginosa*

Ammonia Producers

Proteus miragilis	*Proteus vulgaris*
Brevibacterium ammoniagenes	

Facultative dermatophytes

Trichophyton gypseum	*Trichophyton interdigital*
Trichophyton rubrum	*Epidermophyton floecosum*
Candida albicans	

Fungi

Aspergillus niger	*Aspergillus oryzae*
Aspergillus terreus	*Penicillium citrium*
Penicillium funiculosum	*Penicillium* sp.
Penicillium rogueforti	*Pullularia pullulans*
Candida albicans	

• *Gozarte* **An Herbal Formula (from the Columbian rainforest)**

Gozarte is a natural herbal mixture of 500 mg. of *Artemesia annus* (Vera) conjugated to 100 mg. of Gossypol. This combination provides an extremely potent broad spectrum anti-parasitic agent. Gozarte is absorbed rapidly from the gastro-intestinal tract into the bloodstream and is active locally and systemically within minutes after swallowing. It is a very effective agent and can be given concomitantly or independently with other products such as Neo-Pararte, Udarte and other parasite fighters. Gram for gram, Gozarte is 10 times more potent than Flagyl and Paramomcin and 1000 times more potent than Diodoquin, with no side effects. It is a broad spectrum anti-protozoal agent specifically effective against *Entamoeba histolytica, Giardia lamblia and Dientamoeba fragiles,* malaria, tapeworms, fungicidal activity and Herpes II. Refer to Parasite Elimination Kits A1, B1 or C1, depending on your body weight.

In a chronic case of parasite infestation, Neo-Pararte or Udarte should be taken in conjunction with Gozarte and the other parasite fighters for maximum results. Refer to Parasite Elimination Kits A3, B3 or C3, or A5, B5 or C5, depending on your body weight.

Adverse reactions are dose dependent and disappear upon discontinuation of the product. Herxheimer (die-off) reaction may occur with any effective parasitic elimination therapy. There are no known side effects. Gozarte is not recommended for pregnant or lactating women.

Take Gozarte with food if you have a history of stomach ulcers. Reduce all anti-oxidant supplements to *no more* than the following daily dosages while taking Gozarte:

Vitamin A - 25,000 units   Iron - Less than 100 mg.
Vitamin C - 1000 mg.   Germanium - 30 mg.
Vitamin E - 400 I.U.

Discontinue all other anti-oxidants while on this program. Anti-oxidants in high dosages reduce the potency of Gozarte, an

Artemesia product, thus making it less effective. Avoid alcoholic and carbonated beverages while taking Gozarte.

• **Neo-Pararte** An Herbal Formula *(from the Columbian rainforest)*

Neo-Pararte is a natural herbal mixture of 400 mg. *Artemesia annua* (Vera) conjugated to both 100 mg. DF-100 (an extract of grapefruit seed) and Lemoncillo 500 mg. This combination is an extremely effective and efficient broad spectrum anti-parasitic agent.

Neo-Pararte is absorbed rapidly from the gastro-intestinal tract into the bloodstream and is active both locally and systemically within one-half hour after taking. It is a very effective agent and can be used concomitantly with products such as Gozarte and other parasite fighters.

In a chronic case of parasite infestation, Neo-Pararte should be taken in conjunction with Gozarte and the other *Healing Within* parasite fighters for maximum results. Refer to Parasite Elimination Kits A3, B3 or C3, depending on your body weight.

Adverse reactions are dose dependent and disappear upon discontinuation of the product. Herxheimer (die-off) reaction may occur with any effective herbal parasitic elimination therapy. There are no known side effects. Neo-Pararte is not recommended for pregnant or lactating women.

Take Neo-Pararte with food if you have a history of stomach ulcers. Reduce all anti-oxidant supplements to *no more* than the following daily dosages while taking Neo-Pararte:

Vitamin A - 25,000 units   Iron - Less than 100 mg.
Vitamin C - 1000 mg.   Germanium - 30 mg.
Vitamin E - 400 I.U.

Discontinue all other anti-oxidants while on this program. Anti-oxidants in high dosages reduce the potency of Neo-Pararte, an Artemesia product, thus making it less effective. Avoid alcoholic and carbonated beverages while taking Neo-Pararte.

• *Udarte* An Herbal Formula *(from the Columbian rainforest)*

Udarte is a natural herbal mixture of *Artemisia annua* (Vera) and AC Factor of plant source (Pringamoza). It is obtained from a Colombian variety of an uticaraceie plant. This combination provides an extremely potent broad spectrum anti-parasitic as well as anti-candida agent. The antichitin element, or AC Factor, destroys the cellular membrane of parasites and yeast with a catastrophic effect on those organisms.

Udarte is absorbed rapidly into the bloodstream and is active locally and systemically within minutes after swallowing. It is a very effective agent and should be taken concomitantly with Gozarte and the other *Healing Within* parasite fighters.

In a chronic case of parasite infestation and candida overgrowth, Udarte should be taken in conjunction with Gozarte and the other *Healing Within* parasitic fighters for maximum results. Refer to Parasite Elimination Kits A5, B5 or C5, depending on your body weight.

Adverse reactions are dose dependent and disappear upon discontinuation of the product. Herxheimer (die off) reaction may occur with an effective herbal parasitic and candida elimination therapy. There are no known side effects. Udarte is not recommended for pregnant or lactating women.

Take Udarte with food if you have a history of stomach ulcers. Reduce all anti-oxidant supplements to *no more* than the following daily dosages while taking Udarte:

Vitamin A - 25,000 units	Iron - Less than 100 mg.
Vitamin C - 1000 mg.	Germanium - 30 mg.
Vitamin E - 400 I.U.	

Discontinue all other anti-oxidants while on this program. Anti-oxidants in high dosages reduce the potency of Udarte, an Artemesia product, thus making it less effective. Avoid alcoholic and carbonated beverages while taking Udarte.

• *Pasaloc* An Herbal Formula *(from the Columbian rainforest)*

Pasaloc is a natural herbal mixture of *E. longitdia colombianensis, Salvia officinalis colombianensis* and *Malva colombianensis* (500 mg. per capsule). These herbs, grown in the rain forests of Colombia, are an extremely effective and efficient broad spectrum systemic anti-parasitic combination. Pasaloc can be used concomitantly with other parasite-fighting herbs.

Note that Pasaloc does *not* contain the herb *Artemesia annua*. Large dosages of oxygen-containing products such as Vitamins A, C, E, Iron and Germanium can inhibit the strength and effectiveness of Artemesia based products such as Gozarte, Udarte and Neo-Pararte. Thus, if you wish to take large amounts of anti-oxidants and oxygen-containing products while on the Parasite Elimination Program, your choice should be Pasaloc, since it doesn't contain *Artemesia annua*. Refer to Parasite Elimination Kits A2, B2 and C2, depending on your body weight.

In a chronic case of parasite infestation, Pasaloc should be taken in conjunction with Padapco and the other *Healing Within* parasite fighters for maximum results. Refer to Parasite Elimination Kits A4, B4 or C4, depending on your body weight.

Adverse reactions are dose dependent and disappear upon discontinuation of the product. Herxheimer (die-off) reaction may occur with any effective herbal parasitic elimination therapy. There are no known side effects to Pasaloc. Pasaloc is not recommended for pregnant or lactating women. Take Pasaloc with food if you have a history of stomach ulcers. Avoid alcoholic and carbonated beverages while taking this product.

• *Padapco* An Herbal Formula *(from the Columbian rainforest)*

Padapco is a natural herbal mixture of equal amounts of *Daphentin a.d., Axantorryzia colombianensis* and *Citrus paradisi* (500 mg. per capsule). These herbs, grown in the rain forests of

Colombia, are an extremely effective and efficient broad spectrum systemic anti-parasitic combination. Padapco can be used concomitantly with other parasite-fighting herbs.

Note that Padapco does *not* contain the herb *Artemesia annua*. Large dosages of oxygen-containing products such as Vitamins A, C, E, Iron and Germanium can inhibit the strength and effectiveness of Artemesia based products such as Gozarte, Udarte and Neo-Pararte. Thus, if you wish to take large amounts of anti-oxidants and oxygen-containing products while on the Parasite Elimination Program, your choice should be Padapco, since it doesn't contain *Artemesia annua.*

In a chronic case of parasite infestation, Padapco should be taken in conjunction with Pasaloc and the other *Healing Within* parasite fighters for maximum results. Refer to Parasite Elimination Kits A4, B4 or C4, depending on your body weight.

Adverse reactions are dose dependent and disappear upon discontinuation of the product. Herxheimer (die-off) reaction may occur with any effective parasitic elimination therapy. There are no known side effects to Padapco. Padapco is not recommended for pregnant or lactating women. Take Padapco with food if you have a history of stomach ulcers. Avoid alcoholic and carbonated beverages while taking this product.

Mon Paradise An Herbal Formula *(from the Columbian rainforest)*

Mon Paradise is a natural herbal mixture of crystals of Amazonian *C. Paradisi,* total natural powderized blended species of *Malvaceae* (Gossypol-containing.)

Each capsule contains 500 mg. of active 100% natural ingredients. This herbal combination has broad spectrum effects and can be used in conjunction with other herbal combinations.

In a chronic case of parasite infestation Mon Paradise should be taken in conjunction with other *Healing Within* herbal combinations.

44

It is absorbed rapidly from the gastro intestinal tract into the bloodstream and is active locally and systemically within one-half hour after taking.

Adverse reactions are dose dependent and disappear upon discontinuation of the product. Herxheimer (die-off) reaction may occur with any effective herbal parasitic elimination therapy.

There are no known side effects. Mon Paradise is not recommended for pregnant or lactating women. Take Mon Paradise with food if you have a history of stomach ulcers. Avoid alcohol and carbonated beverages while taking Mon Paradise.

Para-Citro An Herbal Formula *(from the Columbian rainforest)*

Para-Citro is a natural herbal mixture of conjugated 100 mg. of grapefruit extract by 200 mg. of *Colombianensis citronella* powder.

Each capsule contains 500 mg. of active 100% natural ingredients. This herbal combination has broad spectrum effects and can be used in conjunction with other herbal combinations.

In a chronic case of parasite infestation Para-Citro should be taken in conjunction with other *Healing Within* herbal combinations.

Para-Citro is absorbed rapidly from the gastro intestinal tract into the bloodstream and is active locally and systemically within one-half hour after taking.

Adverse reactions are dose dependent and disappear upon discontinuation of the product. Herxheimer (die-off) reaction may occur with any effective herbal parasitic elimination therapy.

There are no known side effects. Para-Citro is not recommended for pregnant or lactating women. Take Para-Citro with food if you have a history of stomach ulcers. Avoid alcohol and carbonated beverages while taking Para-Citro.

Phyll-Martin An Herbal Formula (from the Columbian rainforest)

Phyll-Martin is a natural herbal mixture of *Phyllantus amarus, Phyllantus accuminates, Martin galvis,* and *Phylantus nuris.*

Each capsule contains 500 mg. of active 100% natural ingredients. This herbal combination has broad spectrum effects and can be used in conjunction with other *Healing Within* herbal combinaton. It has particular action against *Blastocystis hominis* and other difficult to treat protozoa.

It is absorbed rapidly from the gastro intestinal tract into the bloodstream and is active locally and systemically within one-half hour after taking.

Adverse reactions are dose dependent and disappear upon discontinuation of the product. Herxheimer (die-off) reaction may occur with any effective herbal parasitic elimination therapy.

There are no known side effects. Phyll-Martin is not recommended for pregnant or lactating women. Take Phyll-Martin with food if you have a history of stomach ulcers. Avoid alcohol and carbonated beverages while taking Phyll-Martin.

Biocidin

Most herbal extracts are manufactured at a 4:1 or 6:1 concentration. The ratio of herbs in Biocidin is 12:1, making it an exceptionally potent formulation. One fluid ounce of Biocidin contains a 6 to 8 week supply.

Through in-vitro testing, Greak Smokies Diagnostic Laboratories in Asheville, North Carolina and C. C. & M. Laboratories in Portland, Oregon have found this gentain formula, Biocidin, to have unusually broad-spectrum activity.

Biocidin Ingredients

- Chlorophyll
- *Frasera carolinensis*
- *Ferula galbanum*
- Allicin
- Fumaria
- *Hydrastis canadensis*
- Sanguinaria
- *Villa rubris*
- *Impatiens pallida*
- *Gentiana campestris*
- *Hypericum perforatum*
- Garlic

46

Biotonic

Biotonic contains hand selected, all natural ingredients of the highest grade, which have been extracted for maximum bio-availability.

Biotonic Ingredients

- *Radix Astragalus*
- *Frasera carolinensis*
- *Ferula galbanum*
- Allicin
- Fumaria
- *Hydrastis canadensis*
- Sanguinaria
- *Villa rubris*
- *Impatiens pallida*
- *Gentiana campestris*
- *Hypericum perforatum*
- Garlic

Recommendations

See pages 67-69 for an itemization of all the products in the *Healing Within* Parasite Elimination Kits. A price list for these kits, as well as individual items, is on page 71.

If you have a protozoa problem I would suggest you use Kits A3, B3 or C3 (depending on your body weight), all of which contain Gozarte and Neo-Pararte. If you have protozoa as well as candida (or a history of candida problems), use Kits A5, B5 or C5 (depending on your body weight). However, you must reduce anti-oxidant supplements such as Vitamins A, C, E, Iron and Germanium. If you wish to continue taking large dosages of these supplements, use Kits A4, B4 or C4 (depending on your body weight), all of which contain Pasaloc and Padapco. Anti-oxidant supplements will not interfere with the effectiveness of Pasaloc and Padapco.

Another excellent choice for Parasite Elimination would be Kits A, B, or C 6, 7, and 8. For these 60 day programs the Echinacea, Shitake, and Intestinalis products have been omitted. Biocidin and Biotonic have been added to these programs (see page 5 for a description of both products.) These Kits are suggested where the immune system may not need the added support of Echinacea and Shitake mushroom but, by the addition of Biocidin and Biotonic, we present the most effective herbal products available to completely eliminate parasite problems. These products are safe and non-toxic—with no known side effects. Completing one of these programs can contribute to restoring one's health for those plagued with parasites, candida and other immune disorders.

Gozarte, Udarte, Neo-Pararte, Pasaloc, Padapco, Mon Paradise, Para-Citro, and Phyll-Martin work very efficiently; so efficiently, in fact, that they may cause some die-off reaction. Having a colonic irrigation or suspending the program for a day or two (if necessary) will probably relieve the symptoms. You can effectively deal with nausea from die-off reactions, if that occurs, by taking the natural herb Stinging Nettles *(Urtica dioica)*.

• *K-Min*

K-Min is a combination product of elements gathered above the earth and mined from the earth. K-Min will, by ionization, take worms apart; rarely will parasites pass out of the body whole. K-Min is a very effective compound in removing parasites from the intestinal tract. When the intestinal tract is free of parasites, yeast infection will usually clear up. The combination of K-Min and Black Walnut Tincture is effective against fungi, skin infections (due to microscopic parasites), ringworm and larvae from the large intestine.

• *Black Walnut Tincture (green hull)*

Black Walnut Tincture is an herbal fluid that fights parasites throughout the body. When tension is present in the intestinal tract, Black Walnut Tincture is a tremendously soothing healant and is an excellent source of manganese. The elements in Black Walnut Tincture are unsurpassed for helping to strengthen ligaments, tendons and muscles. *Indian Herbology of North America* states that Black Walnut Tincture assists in the healing of acne, burning in the anus, pain over the eyes, gas, headaches, herpes, scurvy, and pain in spleen, as well as syphilis, ulcers, rickets and TB.

• *Castor Oil Capsules*

Castor oil, when encapsulated and frozen, will pass through the stomach and small intestine before dissolving. Freezing castor oil capsules before ingesting totally eliminates the traditional cramping associated with this product, because the capsules dissolve in the ileum, the last three fifths of the small intestine. Here the digestive tract hydrolizes this oil into recinoleic acid, which is harmless to humans but deadly to parasites.

The ileum connects to the cecum by way of the ileocecal valve. The majority of parasites of all kinds will nest in the cecum area (the lower end of the ascending colon where the large bowel begins). This area is warm and moist, providing a plentiful source of fresh food for these poisonous invaders.

Castor oil not only suffocates parasites, but is nature's penetrating oil for colon plaque. When the Castor Oil Capsule is *frozen* it does not act as a laxative. Castor oil is odorless and will not "burp" back.

• *Healing Within Intestinal Cleanser*

Healing Within Intestinal Cleanser pulls mucous, detoxifies, heals, acts as a diuretic, activates flushing of the liver and production of bile, and improves intestinal peristalsis. *Healing Within* Intestinal Cleanser contains the following ingredients:

Bentonite

Bentonite, a totally natural product of Mother Earth, is microscopic and carries a large and varied mineral content. This particular strain of bentonite is unequaled in controlling conditions of diarrhea where virus infections, food allergies, spastic colitis and food poisoning exist. "Bentonite carries a strong negative electron and picks up 12 times its weight in positively charged toxic material from the colon wall for expulsion. The action of bentonite is purely physical and not chemical. Bentonite is used as a treatment of intestinal fermentation (gas), putrefaction, and harmful bacteria as well as parasites." (Medical Annuals of Washington, D.C., Vol.20(6), June, 1961, The Value of Bentonite.)

Wheat Grass

Dr. Birscher, research scientist, calls wheat grass chlorophyll "concentrated Sun Power." Wheat grass also carries a negative electron and picks up eight times its weight in positively charged toxic material from the intestinal walls for expulsion. Wheat grass is known to increase the function of the heart, vascular system, intestines, uterus and lungs. The wheat grass chlorophyll "raises the basic nitrogen exchange and is, therefore, a tonic without comparison." The gentle roughage of wheat grass releases clinging debris from intricate crevices of the bowel.

Apple Fiber

Chemical-free apples make up apple fiber, which is loaded with vitamins, minerals, proteins and life-saving pectin and lipids. Apple fiber gently "brushes" and cleanses the intestinal wall, while the apple seeds provide nitrilosides.

Citrus Pectin and Plantago Avato

These products capture putrefactive bacteria for expulsion. The jelling effect of pectin and plantago avato make them especially advantageous in this formula. The two are invaluable in forming a gentle colloidal mass for capturing and holding in suspension the impacted toxic material pulled from the walls of the colon. Citrus pectin is known for releasing heavy metals, such as mercury and lead, from the cells for expulsion. Citrus pectin is reported to help counteract the effects of radiation, cut cholesterol in blood, and reduce risk of heart attacks.

Herbs

Nature's natural medicines are part of the plan for man's survival. *Healing Within* Intestinal Cleanser contains gentian, golden seal, buckthorn, rhubarb root, cascara sagrada and aloe vera, all well calculated and delicately balanced in proportions essential for the success of the cleanser and detoxifier.

Lactobacillus Acidophilus

Acidophilus is essential for balancing body chemistry. The purpose of acidophilus in this formula is to reinforce the production of healthy bacteria in the colon. Where there is too little acidophilus, gas forms, stools become putrid, and the normal production of Vitamin K is destroyed. When Vitamin K is destroyed, internal hemorrhaging can occur. When folic acid becomes deficient, the body cannot manufacture enough maintenance B-complex to stabilize the nerves, and thus energy levels diminish and halitosis tells the sordid story

• *Latero Flora*

Latero Flora is extremely effective for individuals with gastrointestinal disturbances, food allergies and candidiasis hypersensitivity syndrome. Latero Flora normalizes the flora in the human digestive tract, aids in digestion and toxin elimination, and discourages the growth of yeast, fungi and other pathogenic microorganisms. Latero Flora restores the original, desirable bacterial balance to human intestines, thus improving many immuno-suppressed conditions.

Luc DeSchepper, M.D., Ph.D., C.A. studied the "before and after" symptoms of 1,500 patients suffering from chronic fatigue, along with a wide variety of immuno-suppressive symptoms. Dr. DeSchepper made his report in the *Townsend Letter for Doctors*: "Latero Flora has shown significant effectiveness in improving and in many cases eliminating gastrointestinal symptoms and food sensitivities, while enhancing the patient's digestive capacities . . . I am convinced that Latero Flora will play a very important role in fighting the scourge of this century — the suppression of the immune system."

Immune System Strengtheners

The immune system is one of the most complex systems of the human body. Until recently, researchers, scientists and physicians have had little understanding of the structure and function of this system. The basic components are the lymphatic system, white blood cells and their specialized groups, and the antibody mechanisms of the specialized organs.

Scientists are gaining a better understanding of the immune system and what it takes to biochemically aid and support its function. Many of these biochemical components are found in valuable herbs and botanical extracts which contain nutrients that are essential in nourishing the glands that regulate the function and detoxification of the immune system.

• *Echinacea*

One of the most outstanding herbs for strengthening the immune system is *Echinacea angustifolia*. Studies in Europe and America have shown that the chemical compounds in Echinacea have anti-inflammatory action while stimulating the healing of wounds. Echinacea has also been shown to stimulate white blood cells and lymphocytes, making it effective against viral and bacterial infections. Echinacea is effective internally or externally, and has no side effects. Parasite Elimination Kits contain a 6-week supply.

• *Shitake Mushroom Capsules*

For centuries in China and Japan, shitake mushrooms have been recognized as a nutritious food and highly esteemed as a home remedy for many ailments. Shitake Mushroom Capsules exhibit a wide spectrum of beneficial effects on the immune system, and are anti-viral, anti-fungal, anti-inflammatory as well as anti-protozoal. They have been known to lower cholesterol and are an excellent candida fighter. Echinacea and Shitake will help to strengthen the immune system and reduce fatigue associated with parasitic problems. *Healing Within* Parasite Elimination Kits contain a 6-week supply.

• *Acidophilus*

Taking an Acidophilus culture during this 60-day program is highly recommended, as it will restore the good bacteria that have been destroyed by antibiotics and parasitic infestation. DDS Acidophilus is capable of producing B vitamins and reducing cholesterol. It helps with food digestion, especially dairy products, and is a natural antibiotic. DDS Acidophilus has been found to help inhibit the following organisms as well as retard the growth of *Candida albicans* (yeast infections).

Bacillus subtilis	*Bacillus cereus*
Bacillus stearothermophilus liquifaciens	*Streptococcus faecalis* var.
Streptococcus lactis	*Lactobacillus lactis*
Lactobacillus casei	*Lactobacillus plantarum*
Lactobacillus leichmannii	*Sarcina lutea*
Serratia marcescens	*Proteus vulgaris*
Escherichia coli	*Salmonella typhosa*
Salmonella schottmuelleri	*Shigella dysenteriae*
Shigella paradysenteriae	*Pseudomonas fluorescens*
Pseudomonas aeruginosa	Staphylococcus aureus
Klebsiella pneumoniae	Vibrio comma

Post-Program Maintenance

• *Intestinalis Herbal Cleanser*

Intestinalis is an excellent combination of 22 herbs to help maintain and protect the intestinal tract from reinfestation after you have completed the *Healing Within* 60-Day Parasite Elimination Program. Intestinalis is both an anti-parasitic and anti-candida agent, as well as a soothing tonic for the intestinal tract.

Parasite Elimination Kit Recommendations

Kit	Body Weight
A	Less than 100 lbs.
B	100-175 lbs.
C	More than 175 lbs.

If you have or suspect that you have parasites:

Kit A3, B3 or C3 with Gozarte and Neo-Pararte	Reduce anti-oxidants to the amounts in the last chart below*
OR	
Kit A4, B4 or C4 with Pasaloc and Padapco	Reduction of anti-oxidants is not required with these products

If you have parasites *and* candida overgrowth:

Kit A5, B5 or C5 with Gozarte and Udarte	Reduce anti-oxidants to the amounts in the last chart below*

If you have parasites AND your immune system has not been depleted:

Kit A6 or A8, B6 or B8, C6 or C8	Reduce anti-oxidants to the amounts in the last chart below*
OR	
Kit A7, B7 or C7	Reduction of anti-oxidants is not required with these products

* Reduce anti-oxidants to *no more* than the following amounts daily:

Vitamin A	25,000 units
Vitamin C	1000 mg.
Vitamin E	400 I.U.
Iron	Less than 100 mg.
Germanium	30 mg.
All other anti-oxidants	Discontinue while on program

Letters from
Satisfied
Clients

Cora Scott
Amesbury, MA 01913

May 28, 1991

Stanley Weinberger
Healing Within
P.O. Box 1013
Larkspur, CA 94977-1013

Dear Stan:

I'm sorry to have taken so long to let you know about the effects of your parasite program. I wanted to observe myself for awhile in order to figure out where my various symptoms were coming from. What I learned was very interesting.

First of all, your program was very effective for getting my eliminations back to normal. For the first time in many years I am having regular bowel movements of a sort that I have not seen since I was a young adult, without any help from intestinal cleansers. Second, I no longer experience those very unpleasant feelings of internal congestion which seemed like some kind of chronic infection. In addition, the chest infection that plagued me for about one and a half years is gone.

These days I am feeling very well (although I have not yet regained all the weight I lost) because I am careful about what I eat. I want to tell you again how deeply grateful I am to you for making your products available to those of us who become ill and would otherwise have nowhere to turn for help because there is so little understanding of these problems within the medical profession. May all your ways prosper!

Yours sincerely,

Cora Scott

Stanley Weinberger
Colon Health Center
84 Berkeley Ave.
San Anselmo, CA 94960

Dear Mr. Weinberger:

I'm pleased to tell you that I highly endorse both your Parasite and Candida eradication programs. Prior to treatment at Colon Health Center, I had both conditions at the same time. My health was so severely affected I could not be employed, not even part-time. The nausea, pain, dizziness, mental disorientation and respiratory distress transformed me into a socially isolated semi-invalid who left the house only twice a week when absolutely necessary to go to the bank or grocery store. And sometimes I had to delegate even those few chores to sympathetic friends, I was that weak! And I looked as terrible as I felt, as I also had a lot of insomnia.

After four years of illness, your programs did an excellent job of turning my situation around and bringing back normal body functioning. Since my case was extreme and stubborn, other programs failed me. Yours did not. Your approach towards eradicating these incapacitating health scourges is the most intensive I've used. Congratulations!

Sincerely,

Nell Roche
Santa Rosa, CA

June 15, 1991

Dear Mr. Weinberger:

I wanted to write to let you know how much I appreciate your efforts. For more than two years I was going to doctors, acupuncturists, homeopaths and herbalists in hopes of finding relief from my illness. Some of the treatments, in particular the acupuncture, seemed to help relieve my symptoms, but none were capable of providing more than temporary relief.

Diagnosed two years ago by my doctor as "having had" the Epstein-Barr virus, he indicated that it wasn't even possible to tell if the virus was still affecting me. Even it if was, he said, there was no treatment.

I am now certain, after your treatment, that while Epstein-Barr may not have been my immediate problem, it likely was the thing that allowed a parasitic infection to get a foothold in my system. The result: insomnia, hypoglycemic-type symptoms, weight loss, diarrhea, fatigue and nervousness.

I found the health center physicians almost totally ignorant about parasitic infections, and even incapable of diagnosing them properly. I tried your Parasite Elimination Program because I suspected that parasites might be the cause, but in all honesty I wasn't totally convinced. And, in the middle of the treatment, when my doubts surfaced, I was grateful for your reassurance during our phone conversations. The eventual results justify your assurance.

The change has been dramatic. I'm back to pursuing my avocation – photography – and I'm able to run errands without worrying about having an "attack" while out. In short, only two weeks after finishing the treatment, I have begun to feel "normal" for the first time in years. It's so great to see the light again. Hooray!

Many thanks,
Gay Marshall

November 13, 1992

Dear Stanley,

Eight years ago, at age 40, I retired as a Senior Army Officer, after twenty-two years of service. During the transition years the state of my health became the focus of my life. As I became a vegetarian, yogi and tantra yogi, I detoxified, colon cleansed and was therapied. I was Rolf'd, Heller'd, and Trager'd. Whatever was new and hot was next. I was hooked. "Hello, my name is John, and I'm a healing addict."

So it was, several years later, that I arrived at your door with my chin on my chest and deeply exhausted. The great reserve of youthful vibrance and genetic strength that had seen me through the trials of my life was depleted. I was in breakdown.

The information that you shared enabled me to begin to recall the jungles and countrysides to which, as a special forces soldier, I had been sent; and the reactions of my body, to the foods and liquids offered to me, made sense. Finally I was clear. I still had parasites! The previous treatments had been ineffective; and my immune system was seriously inhibited. Thankfully my genetic predisposition for health supported me beyond the military. The thought of being in breakdown, and at the mercy of the Army Medical Corps is too horrific to ponder.

I have completed the Parasite Elimination Program and although my immune system is just beginning to heal, the changes are dramatic. I require less food and sleep for the same lifestyle. The bloating that I once experienced is gone. And, my body is more fit and toned.

Lastly, it was you, Stanley, the person and storehouse of knowledge, that made my choice to do the program an easy one. I sincerely appreciate your being there with me in those moments that were most challenging. Thanks for your support and love.

Warm regards,

John Freedom
Corte Madera, CA

June 22, 1994

To whom it may concern:

As a 27-year employee of a major airline, I found myself exposed, through travel to many exotic ports, to a frightening array of parasitic creatures. For 6 years, I found out the full extent of what traditional medicine did not know. I almost accepted as normal the fatigue, infections, antibiotics, allergies, yeast problems and indigestion that I regularly experienced. Finally, a year ago, I visited Stan Weinberger's Healing Within clinic and took the full parasitic treatment. This was followed by the candida program. I now have a major reduction of all the above-mentioned problems, and the progress is continuing. And while certain portions of the program have required strict dietary restrictions and some discipline, the results are without question worth every effort.

Sincerely,

Loni Blissard
Honolulu, Hawaii

December 18, 1992

Stan Weinberger

Dear Stan:

I just wanted you to know how much I appreciate the help you have given me with my health. It is now about 4 months since I completed the parasite cleanse and I am steadily doing better.

I'm continuing to take the Dioxychlor, but am not really sure that I have a candida problem any more. After years of a major candida problem, it finally seems to be disappearing. I figure I'll stop taking the Dioxychlor on a gradual basis and see what happens

I continue to gain in energy and well-being. For the last seven years I have had to go weekly to the chiropractor to stay in adjustment and keep away migraine headaches. Since completing the parasite cleanse and about 2 months into the Dioxychlor program, I was able to stop going to the chiropractor regularly and have only gone once in the last 3 months. There have been days I have felt totally healthy and then I get very excited because I get the idea of what it would be like to have no body problems at all. It seems clear that I am moving toward that and to an end to the distractions that the body has been these last ten years.

Best wishes for the coming year,

Alexandra Hopkins
North Hollywood, CA

September 14, 1991

In 1991, I found myself depleted, fatigued, and plagued with digestive problems, chronic bloating, gas, and you name it. After trying several different therapies and approaches, Stanley Weinberger finally nailed it: parasites.

"Parasites!" I said, "But . . . ." Stanley then explained it all to me.

"How can you possibly get rid of Candida, Epstein-Barr, the gas and bloating and digestive problems if you don't address your condition on the ground level?" he said. "The invasion of the parasites has lowered your immune system, creating the environment for the other conditions to enter into your weakened system. Then one thing led to another. You have to get rid of the parasites first, and then the other conditions will either disappear, improve, or at least you will be able to address them effectively."

I was so grateful to finally get the answers I had been searching for, as nobody had been able to explain my condition accurately to me. I immediately began Stanley's 60-Day Parasite Elimination Program.

There were days when I felt awful, and other days when I began to see the light at the end of the tunnel and felt my energy and enthusiasm returning. Whenever I felt really bad and clogged up, I would take a colonic and always felt relieved. And there were moments when I resisted the program. But with a call to Stanley and a few encouraging words from my coach, my doubts and fears vanished and I started up again.

I finished the program, and I'm now basically back to normal. Most of my conditions have either disappeared or diminished. Those that remain I can now deal with in a stronger, more cleaned-out state.

Stanley really knows what he is doing, and has the most up-to-date information on the best supplements and herbs to take. He is totally dedicated to healing and helping people all over the country, is impeccable in his practice, and can be trusted to accurately pinpoint the area of concern. He's the best.

Constance Denby
San Anselmo, CA

May 1, 1997
Stanley Weinberger
Healing Within

Dear Mr. Weinberger

I'm sorry to have taken so long to let you know about the effect of your program. I wanted to observe my son because my son was born with Candida. He saw the doctor all the time and all the doctor said it was was Head Conjunction and he always gave my son the same medicine all the time and he got worse. His life changed when I read Mr. Weinberger's book. I called him and I can't believe what he told me. He gave my son some treatment and now my son— he can eat everything he can. Candy, chocolates . . . you know, kids love candy and I want to tell you that I'm pleased with you and thank you. You're the best.

Warm regard,
Teresa Ibarra
Houston, TX

Parasite Elimination Kits and Order Form

60-Day Parasite Elimination Program Kits
— For body weight under 100 lbs. —

KIT A3 — Complete 60-Day Kit   22 Bottles Total — $631.00

1 Black Walnut Tincture (4 ounces each bottle)
2 Castor Oil (180 capsules each bottle)
2 DDS Acidophilus (100 capsules each bottle)
2 Echinacea (90 capsules each bottle)
3 Gozarte (60 capsules each bottle)
2 *Healing Within* Intestinal Cleanser
  (250 capsules each bottle)

1 Intestinalis Herbal Cleanser (60 tblts. each bottle)
2 K-Min (180 capsules each bottle)
2 Latero Flora (60 capsules each bottle)
3 Neo-Pararte (60 capsules each bottle)
2 Shitake Mushrooms (90 capsules each bottle)

KIT A4 — Complete 60-Day Kit   22 Bottles Total — $ 631.00

1 Black Walnut Tincture (4 ounces each bottle)
2 Castor Oil (180 capsules each bottle)
2 DDS Acidophilus (100 capsules each bottle)
2 Echinacea (90 capsules each bottle)
2 *Healing Within* Intestinal Cleanser
  (250 capsules each bottle)

1 Intestinalis Herbal Cleanser (60 tblts. each bottle)
2 K-Min (180 capsules each bottle)
2 Latero Flora (60 capsules each bottle)
3 Padapco (60 capsules each bottle)
3 Pasaloc (60 capsules each bottle)
2 Shitake Mushrooms (90 capsules each bottle)

KIT A5 — Complete 60-Day Kit   22 Bottles Total — $ 631.00

1 Black Walnut Tincture (4 ounces each bottle)
2 Castor Oil (180 capsules each bottle)
2 DDS Acidophilus (100 capsules each bottle)
2 Echinacea (90 capsules each bottle)
3 Gozarte (60 capsules each bottle)
2 *Healing Within* Intestinal Cleanser
  (250 capsules each bottle)

1 Intestinalis Herbal Cleanser (60 tblts. each bottle)
2 K-Min (180 capsules each bottle)
2 Latero Flora (60 capsules each bottle)
2 Shitake Mushrooms (90 capsules each bottle)
3 Udarte (60 capsules each bottle)

KIT A6 — Complete 60-Day Kit   20 Bottles Total — $ 633.00

1 Black Walnut Tincture (4 ounces each bottle)
1 Biocidin (1 ounce, 700 drops each bottle)
2 Biotonic (120 capsules each bottle)
2 Castor Oil (180 capsules each bottle)
2 DDS Acidophilus (100 capsules each bottle)
3 Gozarte (60 capsules each bottle)

2 *Healing Within* Intestinal Cleanser
  (250 capsules each bottle)
2 K-Min (180 capsules each bottle)
2 Latero Flora (60 capsules each bottle)
3 Udarte (60 capsules each bottle)

KIT A7 — Complete 60-Day Kit   20 Bottles Total — $ 633.00

1 Black Walnut Tincture (4 ounces each bottle)
1 Biocidin (1 ounce, 700 drops each bottle)
2 Biotonic (120 capsules each bottle)
2 Castor Oil (180 capsules each bottle)
2 DDS Acidophilus (100 capsules each bottle)
2 *Healing Within* Intestinal Cleanser
  (250 capsules each bottle)

2 K-Min (180 capsules each bottle)
2 Latero Flora (60 capsules each bottle)
3 Padapco (60 capsules each bottle)
3 Pasaloc (60 capsules each bottle)

KIT A8 — Complete 60-Day Kit   20 Bottles Total — $ 633.00

1 Black Walnut Tincture (4 ounces each bottle)
1 Biocidin (1 ounce, 700 drops each bottle)
2 Biotonic (120 capsules each bottle)
2 Castor Oil (180 capsules each bottle)
2 DDS Acidophilus (100 capsules each bottle)
3 Gozarte (60 capsules each bottle)

2 *Healing Within* Intestinal Cleanser
  (250 capsules each bottle)
2 K-Min (180 capsules each bottle)
2 Latero Flora (60 capsules each bottle)
3 Neopararte (60 capsules each bottle)

**Detailed instructions for taking the products will be enclosed in your
Parasite Elimination Program Kit.**

60-Day Parasite Elimination Program Kits
— For body weight 100-175 lbs. —

KIT B3 — Complete 60-Day Kit   23 Bottles Total — $644.00

1 Black Walnut Tincture (4 ounces each bottle)
3 Castor Oil (180 capsules each bottle)
2 DDS Acidophilus (100 capsules each bottle)
2 Echinacea (90 capsules each bottle)
3 Gozarte (60 capsules each bottle)
2 *Healing Within* Intestinal Cleanser
  (250 capsules each bottle)

1 Intestinalis Herbal Cleanser (60 tblts. each bottle)
2 K-Min (180 capsules each bottle)
2 Latero Flora (60 capsules each bottle)
3 Neo-Pararte (60 capsules each bottle)
2 Shitake Mushrooms (90 capsules each bottle)

KIT B4 — Complete 60-Day Kit   23 Bottles Total — $ 644.00

1 Black Walnut Tincture (4 ounces each bottle)
3 Castor Oil (180 capsules each bottle)
2 DDS Acidophilus (100 capsules each bottle)
2 Echinacea (90 capsules each bottle)
2 *Healing Within* Intestinal Cleanser
  (250 capsules each bottle)

1 Intestinalis Herbal Cleanser (60 tblts. each bottle)
2 K-Min (180 capsules each bottle)
2 Latero Flora (60 capsules each bottle)
3 Padapco (60 capsules each bottle)
3 Pasaloc (60 capsules each bottle)
2 Shitake Mushrooms (90 capsules each bottle)

KIT B5 — Complete 60-Day Kit   23 Bottles Total — $ 644.00

1 Black Walnut Tincture (4 ounces each bottle)
3 Castor Oil (180 capsules each bottle)
2 DDS Acidophilus (100 capsules each bottle)
2 Echinacea (90 capsules each bottle)
3 Gozarte (60 capsules each bottle)
2 *Healing Within* Intestinal Cleanser
  (250 capsules each bottle)

1 Intestinalis Herbal Cleanser (60 tblts. each bottle)
2 K-Min (180 capsules each bottle)
2 Latero Flora (60 capsules each bottle)
2 Shitake Mushrooms (90 capsules each bottle)
3 Udarte (60 capsules each bottle)

KIT B6 — Complete 60-Day Kit   21 Bottles Total — $ 646.00

1 Black Walnut Tincture (4 ounces each bottle)
1 Biocidin (1 ounce, 700 drops each bottle)
2 Biotonic (120 capsules each bottle)
3 Castor Oil (180 capsules each bottle)
2 DDS Acidophilus (100 capsules each bottle)
3 Gozarte (60 capsules each bottle)

2 *Healing Within* Intestinal Cleanser
  (250 capsules each bottle)
2 K-Min (180 capsules each bottle)
2 Latero Flora (60 capsules each bottle)
3 Udarte (60 capsules each bottle)

KIT B7 — Complete 60-Day Kit   21 Bottles Total — $ 646.00

1 Black Walnut Tincture (4 ounces each bottle)
1 Biocidin (1 ounce, 700 drops each bottle)
2 Biotonic (120 capsules each bottle)
3 Castor Oil (180 capsules each bottle)
2 DDS Acidophilus (100 capsules each bottle)
2 *Healing Within* Intestinal Cleanser
  (250 capsules each bottle)

2 K-Min (180 capsules each bottle)
2 Latero Flora (60 capsules each bottle)
3 Padapco (60 capsules each bottle)
3 Pasaloc (60 capsules each bottle)

KIT B8 — Complete 60-Day Kit   21 Bottles Total — $ 646.00

1 Black Walnut Tincture (4 ounces each bottle)
1 Biocidin (1 ounce, 700 drops each bottle)
2 Biotonic (120 capsules each bottle)
3 Castor Oil (180 capsules each bottle)
2 DDS Acidophilus (100 capsules each bottle)
3 Gozarte (60 capsules each bottle)

2 *Healing Within* Intestinal Cleanser
  (250 capsules each bottle)
2 K-Min (180 capsules each bottle)
2 Latero Flora (60 capsules each bottle)
3 Neopararte (60 capsules each bottle)

**Detailed instructions for taking the products will be enclosed in your
Parasite Elimination Program Kit.**

60-Day Parasite Elimination Program Kits
— For body weight over 175 lbs. —

KIT C3 — Complete 60-Day Kit — 25 Bottles Total — $677.00

1 Black Walnut Tincture (4 ounces each bottle)
4 Castor Oil (180 capsules each bottle)
2 DDS Acidophilus (100 capsules each bottle)
2 Echinacea (90 capsules each bottle)
3 Gozarte (60 capsules each bottle)
3 *Healing Within* Intestinal Cleanser
  (250 capsules each bottle)
1 Intestinalis Herbal Cleanser (60 tblts. each bottle)
2 K-Min (180 capsules each bottle)
2 Latero Flora (60 capsules each bottle)
3 Neo-Pararte (60 capsules each bottle)
2 Shitake Mushrooms (90 capsules each bottle)

KIT C4 — Complete 60-Day Kit — 25 Bottles Total — $ 677.00

1 Black Walnut Tincture (4 ounces each bottle)
4 Castor Oil (180 capsules each bottle)
2 DDS Acidophilus (100 capsules each bottle)
2 Echinacea (90 capsules each bottle)
3 *Healing Within* Intestinal Cleanser
  (250 capsules each bottle)
1 Intestinalis Herbal Cleanser (60 tblts. each bottle)
2 K-Min (180 capsules each bottle)
2 Latero Flora (60 capsules each bottle)
3 Padapco (60 capsules each bottle)
3 Pasaloc (60 capsules each bottle)
2 Shitake Mushrooms (90 capsules each bottle)

KIT C5 — Complete 60-Day Kit — 25 Bottles Total — $ 677.00

1 Black Walnut Tincture (4 ounces each bottle)
4 Castor Oil (180 capsules each bottle)
2 DDS Acidophilus (100 capsules each bottle)
2 Echinacea (90 capsules each bottle)
3 Gozarte (60 capsules each bottle)
3 *Healing Within* Intestinal Cleanser
  (250 capsules each bottle)
1 Intestinalis Herbal Cleanser (60 tblts. each bottle)
2 K-Min (180 capsules each bottle)
2 Latero Flora (60 capsules each bottle)
2 Shitake Mushrooms (90 capsules each bottle)
3 Udarte (60 capsules each bottle)

KIT C6 — Complete 60-Day Kit — 23 Bottles Total — $ 679.00

1 Black Walnut Tincture (4 ounces each bottle)
1 Biocidin (1 ounce, 700 drops each bottle)
2 Biotonic (120 capsules each bottle)
4 Castor Oil (180 capsules each bottle)
2 DDS Acidophilus (100 capsules each bottle)
3 Gozarte (60 capsules each bottle)
3 *Healing Within* Intestinal Cleanser
  (250 capsules each bottle)
2 K-Min (180 capsules each bottle)
2 Latero Flora (60 capsules each bottle)
3 Udarte (60 capsules each bottle)

KIT B7 — Complete 60-Day Kit — 23 Bottles Total — $ 679.00

1 Black Walnut Tincture (4 ounces each bottle)
1 Biocidin (1 ounce, 700 drops each bottle)
2 Biotonic (120 capsules each bottle)
4 Castor Oil (180 capsules each bottle)
2 DDS Acidophilus (100 capsules each bottle)
3 *Healing Within* Intestinal Cleanser
  (250 capsules each bottle)
2 K-Min (180 capsules each bottle)
2 Latero Flora (60 capsules each bottle)
3 Padapco (60 capsules each bottle)
3 Pasaloc (60 capsules each bottle)

KIT B8 — Complete 60-Day Kit — 23 Bottles Total — $ 679.00

1 Black Walnut Tincture (4 ounces each bottle)
1 Biocidin (1 ounce, 700 drops each bottle)
2 Biotonic (120 capsules each bottle)
4 Castor Oil (180 capsules each bottle)
2 DDS Acidophilus (100 capsules each bottle)
3 Gozarte (60 capsules each bottle)
3 *Healing Within* Intestinal Cleanser
  (250 capsules each bottle)
2 K-Min (180 capsules each bottle)
2 Latero Flora (60 capsules each bottle)
3 Neopararte (60 capsules each bottle)

**Detailed instructions for taking the products will be enclosed in your
Parasite Elimination Program Kit.**

Parasite Elimination Program Order Form

Minimum Order: $25.00

Complete Parasite Elimination Program Kits	Quantity	Price	Total
Kit A3 – (For body weight under 100 lbs.)	_____	631.00	_____
Kit A4 – (For body weight under 100 lbs.)	_____	631.00	_____
Kit A5 – (For body weight under 100 lbs.)	_____	631.00	_____
Kit A6 – (For body weight under 100 lbs.)	_____	633.00	_____
Kit A7 – (For body weight under 100 lbs.)	_____	633.00	_____
Kit A8 – (For body weight under 100 lbs.)	_____	633.00	_____
Kit B3 – (For body weight 100-175 lbs.)	_____	644.00	_____
Kit B4 – (For body weight 100-175 lbs.)	_____	644.00	_____
Kit B5 – (For body weight 100-175 lbs.)	_____	644.00	_____
Kit B6 – (For body weight 100-175 lbs.)	_____	646.00	_____
Kit B7 – (For body weight 100-175 lbs.)	_____	646.00	_____
Kit B8 – (For body weight 100-175 lbs.)	_____	646.00	_____
Kit C3 – (For body weight over 175 lbs.)	_____	677.00	_____
Kit C4 – (For body weight over 175 lbs.)	_____	677.00	_____
Kit C5 – (For body weight over 175 lbs.)	_____	677.00	_____
Kit C6 – (For body weight over 175 lbs.)	_____	679.00	_____
Kit C7 – (For body weight over 175 lbs.)	_____	679.00	_____
Kit C8 – (For body weight over 175 lbs.)	_____	679.00	_____

Individual Items

Biocidin (1 fl. oz. per bottle)	_____	65.00	_____
Biotonic (120 capsules per bottle)	_____	23.00	_____
Black Walnut Tincture (4 oz. per bottle)	_____	12.00	_____
Castor Oil Capsules (180 capsules per bottle)	_____	13.00	_____
Consolar (60 capsules per bottle)	_____	45.00	_____
DDS Acidophilus (100 capsules per bottle)	_____	17.00	_____
Echinacea (90 capsules per bottle)	_____	20.00	_____
Gozarte (60 capsules per bottle	_____	55.00	_____
Healing Within Intestinal Cleanser (120 capsules per bottle)	_____	11.00	_____
Healing Within Intestinal Cleanser (250 capsules per bottle)	_____	20.00	_____
Intestinalis Herbal Cleanser (60 tablets per bottle)	_____	29.00	_____
K-Min (180 capsules per bottle)	_____	14.00	_____
Latero Flora (60 capsules per bottle)	_____	26.00	_____
Neem Leaf (60 capsules, 500 mg. ea., per bottle)	_____	17.00	_____
Mon Paradise (60 capsules per bottle)	_____	55.00	_____
Neo-Pararte (60 capsules per bottle)	_____	55.00	_____
Padapco (60 capsules per bottle)	_____	55.00	_____
Para-Citro (60 capsules per bottle)	_____	55.00	_____
Pasaloc (60 capsules per bottle)	_____	55.00	_____
Phyll-Martin (60 capsules per bottle)	_____	55.00	_____
Shitake Mushrooms (90 capsules per bottle)	_____	20.00	_____
Stinging Nettles (90 capsules per bottle)	_____	20.00	_____
Udarte (60 capsules per bottle)	_____	55.00	_____
Healing Within: The Complete Guide to Colon Health ...	_____	15.95	_____
Parasites: An Epidemic in Disguise	_____	11.95	_____
Candida Albicans: The Quiet Epidemic	_____	11.95	_____

Minimum Order $25.00
Minimum Shipping Chg. $5.00

TOTAL ORDER _____

California residents add 7.5% tax _____

Each Complete Kit Shipping   FREE

Shipping and Handling for individual items:
Up to $50 add 10% of individual item price; over $50 add 8%. _____
(See next page for detailed Shipping & Product Information)

TOTAL AMOUNT ENCLOSED _____

Healing Within Products, Inc.

P.O. Box 1013 • Larkspur, CA 94977-1013

Orders Only (800)300-7548 • (415) 454- 6677 • Fax only (415) 454-6659

Shipping & Product Information

Call or Fax Your Order: You may call or fax your order only with Visa, MasterCard or American Express to *Healing Within Products*. Business hours are 8:00 a.m. to 5:00 p.m. Pacific Standard Time, Monday through Saturday.

Minimum Order: $25.00 **Minimum Shipping Chage:** $5.00

Shipping Method: Orders are shipped via UPS Ground. For Second Day Blue Label delivery, double the shipping charges. No shipping on Saturdays, Sundays or legal holidays. Visa, MasterCard and American Express orders are shipped on the next working day.

Alaska & Hawaii Shipments: For shipments to Alaska and Hawaii, double the continental U.S. shipping charge. Orders will be sent by U.S. First Class Mail.

Canada Shipments: For shipments to Canada, double the continental U.S. shipping charge. Orders will be sent by U.S. Air Parcel Post.

Overseas & Foreign Shipments: For overseas surface shipments, triple the shipping charge; allow 6 weeks for delivery. For overseas air orders, add five times the continental U.S. shipping charge. *All foreign accounts must send bank certified checks in U.S. dollars; credit cards accepted.*

Prices: Prices are subject to change without notice.

Returns: Any items you wish to return must have been purchased within the past 30 days. You cannot return opened bottles or bottles with defaced labels. All returns will have a 10% handling charge. Returned products will not be accepted without prior approval. Call 800-300-7548 for return authorization number. All returned checks will be charged a $10.00 fee. Return shipments by UPS to *Healing Within Products*, 84 Berkeley Ave., San Anselmo, CA 94960. Return shipments by U.S. Postal Service to *Healing Within Products*, P.O. Box 1013, Larkspur, CA 94977-1013.

Product Storage: We suggest storing your supplements in a cool, dry location. The label will specify if refrigeration is required. These products are for nutritional supplementation only. They are not intended for the mitigation, cure or treatment of any disease or illness. No other use is assumed, implied, intended or permitted.

Fax and telephone orders accepted only with Visa, MasterCard, American Express and Discover. Orders pai with bank checks or money orders payable to *Healing Within Products* are shipped on the next working day Send personal check payable to *Healing Within Products*; **allow 2 weeks for delivery.** No C.O.D. Price subject to change.

Please print clearly:

Name _____ **Day Phone (____)** _____

Address _____ **Eve. Phone (____)** _____

City _____ **State** _____ **Zip** _____

❏ **Visa** ❏ **MasterCard** ❏ **Am. Ex.** ❏ **Discover** **Card #** _____

Expiration Date _____ **Signature** _____

– New Choices for Healing Ourselves –

At last . . . A complete guide to colon health which will be of interest to all health-minded individuals.

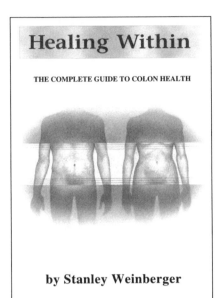

Healing Within

THE COMPLETE GUIDE TO COLON HEALTH

by Stanley Weinberger

Healing Within:
THE COMPLETE GUIDE TO COLON HEALTH
by Stanley Weinberger

For those suffering from yeast problems, constipation, low energy, headaches, digestive problems, and excess weight.

Answers to these and other health related problems are offered in *Healing Within*. Discover how colon therapy, self-help programs and other beneficial health practices can restore vibrant health.

CHC PUBLISHING ISBN 0-9616184-7-7 $15.95

"The road to health is the one that begins with an understanding and commitment to cleanse and detoxify the body, to restore balance, peace and harmony . . ."

Dr. Bernard Jensen, D.C.